THE VICAR OF BAGHDAD

FIGHTING FOR PEACE
IN THE
MIDDLE EAST

Andrew White

MONARCH
BOOKS

OXFORD, UK & GRAND RAPIDS, MICHIGAN

First published in the UK in 2009 by Monarch Books
(a publishing imprint of Lion Hudson plc),
Wilkinson House, Jordan Hill Road, Oxford OX2 8DR.
Tel: +44 (0)1865 302750 Fax: +44 (0)1865 302757
Email: monarch@lionhudson.com
www.lionhudson.com

Reprinted 2009 (twice).

ISBN: 978-1-85424-876-3 (UK)
ISBN: 978-0-8254-6284-9 (USA)

Distributed by:
UK: Marston Book Services Ltd, PO Box 269,
Abingdon, Oxon OX14 4YN;
USA: Kregel Publications, PO Box 2607, Grand Rapids,
Michigan 49501

British Library Cataloguing Data
A catalogue record for this book is available from the British Library.

Printed and bound in United States of America.

DEDICATION

To:

AL, ALAN, JASON, JASON AND PETER

AND ALL MY FRIENDS AT GARDAWORLD:

JEFF, FRANK, JOHN, MARTIN AND TANK,

THE OPS MANAGERS, AND OUR HQ TEAM:

DEL, MICK, BADGER, MARTIN, SEAN, NORRIE,

ROLLIE AND TAFF AND NATALIE,

THE INTERNATIONAL DIRECTOR.

CONTENTS

ACKNOWLEDGEMENTS

This book is about fighting for peace on the front line in some of the most difficult places in the world. It has itself been very difficult to write and edit. Here in Baghdad we do not even have proper internet access, but my editor, Huw Spanner, has persevered to the end and I would like to begin by thanking him.

Then, I would like to thank two of my closest co-workers for peace, both politicians, both men of faith, one a Jew and one a Muslim. Without Rabbi Michael Melchior in Israel and Dr Mowaffak al-Rubaie here in Iraq, there would have been no story to tell.

I would also like to thank all my staff, and especially those who are with me on the front line: in Iraq, the other two corners of 'the Triangle', Samir Raheem al-Soodani and Essam al-Saadi, and in Israel/Palestine Hanna Ishaq.

I thank all my staff in Britain, my trustees and my two boards of advisers, on both sides of the Atlantic; but especially Rosie Watt, my project officer, who has overseen the writing of this book.

Everybody mentioned in these pages is part of the

story and I thank them all. We pray that indeed, one day, peace and reconciliation will come to this region of the world.

Baghdad, 10 October 2008

FOREWORD

During my years at Canterbury I had the privilege of working with Andrew White on a number of occasions. A very special memory stands out when he enlisted my support to bring together the religious leaders of the Middle East region, in order to sign what would become The First Alexandria Declaration of the Religious Leaders of the Holy Land – a momentous document which owed a great deal to Andrew's tireless diplomacy.

Andrew is, truly, one of the most remarkable men I have ever encountered. With intelligence and exuberant energy, allied to a profound personal faith, he would be a force to be reckoned with in any walk of life. But what sets him apart is his capacity to love, and be loved. Children trust him. Crusty old clerics trust him. His staff esteem him. His words, often blunt, are always laced with humour and affection. If one gift above all sets him apart, it is that he is gifted in friendship.

The importance of this book is what it says about the centrality of religion in any discussion of the Middle East. In the secularized West politicians, diplomats and soldiers tend to discount, or underestimate, the importance of faith, but in countries like Iraq it simply cannot be ignored. Andrew White is trusted where few others can win confidence. A man of faith can speak to men of faith.

I wholeheartedly commend this book to your attention. It is an inspirational read.

LORD CAREY OF CLIFTON
(103rd Archbishop of Canterbury)

INTRODUCTION

....

A Quite Unexpected Theatre

WHEN I WAS YOUNG, I certainly had no intention of working in the Middle East. I remember when I was ten telling my teacher I wanted to work in anaesthetics and be a priest. She told me I could only do one thing and I was a Baptist and they didn't have priests. I had already read my first book on anaesthetics – I was a very strange child – and by the time I had finished my schooling seven years later my one desire was to go to St Thomas' Hospital in London and train as an 'operating department practitioner'.

And so I did, and I loved every minute of it. I had no desire ever to leave the medical world – to me it proved to be more wonderful than I had even imagined. But then, late one night, while I was on call for cardiac arrests, I went to pray in the hospital grounds, looking across the river Thames towards Big Ben. I had only recently qualified and I remember thanking God for all he had enabled me to achieve – passing my exams with distinction and getting the job I had always wanted at the hospital I'd always wanted to work at. I thought I should ask what I ought to do next – I hoped the Almighty would want me to just carry on with what I was doing. To my utter amazement, however, I felt very clearly that I was being called to go into the church – in fact, the Church of England.

I had no wish to be ordained, but I went to see Sir Nicholas Rivett-Carnac, the vicar of St Mark's, Kennington, the Anglican church that, like many of the hospital staff, I attended. He was one of the gentlest, wisest and most Spirit-filled men I have ever met, and he encouraged me. In due course, I embarked on the slow process that leads to ordination – and to my surprise found that things moved rather quickly. I also came to experience the glory of God as I never had done before. St Mark's was so alive, and so was the Christian Union at St Thomas'. When I went into the operating theatre early in the morning, the sense of God's presence was so real that often I felt I was in heaven. I spent my days singing his praises. As the weeks went by, my desire to go into the church increased almost by the hour and it wasn't long before all I wanted in life was to be ordained and serve God full-time. Eventually, I went to Ridley Hall, Cambridge and started my training for the Anglican ministry.

I didn't find my theological education easy. Spiritually, I would describe it as something of a 'wilderness experience'. Certainly, it was a good deal harder than my previous training at St Thomas' – at least, until I started studying Judaism under the inspirational professor Nicholas de Lange. This was a subject I felt passionate about. It had fascinated me ever since I was a child: my father had often talked to me about it, and it related to international affairs that had interested and enthused me since my last two years at school. The head of those years, Michael Amos, was one of the most inspiring people I have ever met. Not only did he teach me politics and economics, I would spend my lunch breaks in his study while he went through the serious newspapers with us and talked to us about the world. (I wasn't surprised when, many years later, his daughter became Leader of the House of Lords. In November 2007, when I was awarded the Woolf Institute's Pursuer of Peace Award at the Middle Temple in London, to my delight it was Baroness Amos who presented it to me, and in the presence of her father.)

Studying Judaism gave me the opportunity to take further my interest in international affairs, and in particular my interest in the Middle East. Crucial to the latter was a very English crisis at Cambridge. In 1988, members of the university's inter-collegiate Christian union (known as Ciccu) who were organizing its triennial mission decided to invite evangelists from Jews for Jesus to take part, to try to convert Jewish students. This caused a great deal of resentment among the practising Jews, who asked me to intervene. I was known to both sides and trusted and respected by both – by Ciccu's evangelicals because I was studying at a conservative evangelical college, and because the chair of their mission committee was a good friend of mine (indeed, in due course he was to be my best man!), and by the Jews because I regularly attended Cambridge's Orthodox synagogue and prayed there in Hebrew alongside them.

I told my fellow Christians that trying to persuade people to change their religion is a very dangerous undertaking, but in any event it can be done only if you form a relationship with them. The outcome was that Ciccu went ahead, very carefully, with its evangelistic meeting; but subsequently Jewish and Christian students got together to set up a society called Cambridge University Jews and Christians (or Cujac). This soon became a branch of the Council of Christians and Jews (CCJ), and it was only a matter of time before I found myself chairing the young leadership section of the International Council of Christians and Jews. I worked closely with Sir Sigmund Sternberg, the chair of the ICCJ, and learned a lot from him.

As part of my course at Cambridge, I spent some of my final year in Jerusalem, at the Hebrew University and an Ultra-Orthodox Jewish *yeshiva* or seminary. This was a life-shaping experience, totally different from anything else I had ever encountered. It was the first time I had engaged seriously with another faith tradition – a tradition, moreover, that was the foundation of my own religion. Originally,

I had gone there to study the role of Israel – the people, the land and finally the state – in Christian thought; but I was challenged by seeing at first hand how these Jews practised their faith. So much of their religion was concerned with what they did rather than what they believed – quite the opposite from most Christianity. I had always been taught, by people who had very little understanding of it, that Judaism is all about legalism; but what I observed was that actually the 613 *mitzvot*, or commandments, had one purpose only: to please God.

At the same time, I also got to know well several Islamic leaders in Jerusalem, and so my study of Islam began.

On a second visit to Jerusalem, between my graduation from Cambridge and my ordination, I was instructed by an Ultra-Orthodox rabbi to go and see a woman known as Sister Ruth Heflin, who ran a very charismatic and rather American church called the Mount Zion Fellowship. She proved to be the most forceful person I have ever met. Indeed, I was scared of her. At the end of the first meeting I attended, in her house in East Jerusalem, she came up to me and started to prophesy over me. She had never met me before and knew nothing about me, but she declared that my calling in life was to 'seek the peace of Jerusalem and the Middle East'. At that stage, I couldn't make any sense of this (and I certainly had no inkling that 'the Middle East' might include Iraq) but what I did understand was that her home was filled with the glory of God as I had never experienced it before.

Back in England, I was ordained in 1990 in a wonderful service at Southwark Cathedral and then started work as a curate, or assistant minister, at St Mark's Church, Battersea Rise in south London. It was at this time that I got married to the most wonderful – and most tolerant – woman I have ever met. I was preaching one day when I looked down from the pulpit and saw her for the first time. I liked what I saw so much that afterwards I went up to her and, even though I knew nothing about her, asked if she would help me to organize a mission. Six weeks later, I asked Caroline to marry me.

Our wedding was conducted by Donald Coggan, a former archbishop of Canterbury, who had become my mentor in life. Every time we met, he would say when we parted: 'Don't take care, take risks!' I have never forgotten those words.

My involvement in Jewish-Christian relations continued. (So, indeed, did my work in anaesthetics, though now more as a hobby. Each week on my day off I went to St Thomas' to work as a volunteer. I doubt very much that that would be allowed today.) I regularly travelled overseas, and increasingly to the Middle East. I also deepened my acquaintance with Islam – initially in Africa, in Kenya and Nigeria for example, after the ICCJ had set up its Abrahamic Forum to promote interreligious dialogue between all three of the great monotheistic faiths. It was clear to me that if I was going to play a role in the Middle East I had to understand Islam as well as Judaism. To the surprise of my vicar, I had regular audiences with the Pope to brief him on my work, and we enjoyed a close relationship – I even took Caroline to meet him on one occasion. I liked him so much. As a Strict and Particular Baptist I had been brought up to think of the Vatican as the home of the Antichrist, but I had learned to respect Catholics for the certainty of their faith, and I had also come to believe that godliness matters more than doctrinal correctness (and not only in Christians).

After three years, I moved a mile down the road to become priest-in-charge of the Church of the Ascension, Balham Hill. The congregation was struggling, but it was a wonderful mix of black and white and rich and poor, and at times the glory of God came down there. I was very involved in the local community and eventually was voted onto Wandsworth Borough Council, where in due course I became chair of social services. Meanwhile, I was still chairing the young leadership section of the ICCJ, and by this stage we had also created an active branch of that section in the British CCJ, which was led by another great Jewish friend, Paul Mendel. I didn't know what God was preparing me for, and yet I was receiving an excellent grounding in the fundamentals of international relations and reconciliation.

At St Mark's, my vicar had told me off for being away so much, but now as a vicar myself I travelled all the more. I limited myself to being absent no more than one Sunday in six, but that still meant I could go abroad for almost two weeks at a time. I went back and forth to the Holy Land and the Holy See, and also became ever more involved in the Islamic world. In 1994, jointly with Lord Coggan, I was given the Sir Sigmund Sternberg Award for my 'sustained contribution to the furtherance of interreligious understanding'. I have won many other prizes since then, but none has meant as much to me as the one I shared with him.

Then, one day in 1998, having been at the Church of the Ascension for not quite five years, my bishop, Roy Williamson, suggested that I should apply for the job as canon in charge of international ministry at Coventry Cathedral. At the age of 33 I was barely old enough for such a senior position, but he encouraged me to apply anyway, and to my surprise I was appointed and was soon installed. The cathedral of St Michael's, Coventry is a wonderful place, with an extraordinary history of taking risks for the sake of reconciliation. Moreover, I was succeeding Paul Oestreicher, a truly great man whom I had long admired from afar. Nonetheless, leaving the Church of the Ascension was one of the hardest things I have ever had to do. I loved those people so much, and when I had to tell them I was going I broke down in tears.

My enthusiasm for my new job was undiminished by the discovery that I had multiple sclerosis, a degenerative disease for which there is no known cure. I had gone to see my doctor because I was suffering from double vision and my balance was going. He put me in touch with the local hospital and they admitted me for five weeks. When they told me I had MS, I was upset, of course, but not for long, because my second son, Jacob, was born later that very day. (We called him Aaron at first, but we changed his name the next day. He didn't look like an Aaron.) I was aware of how great a handicap my condition might prove to be, but I am quite an optimist and my temperament as well as my faith averted any kind of spiritual crisis. My new employers didn't know whether I would be able to travel any more, but they realized that there was no point trying to tell me what to do. As for my doctor, he assured me: 'The wonderful thing is, we have a hospice here especially for people with MS.' That really made me laugh.

It soon was clear that if I and my new colleagues were really to help to bring peace to the world, we needed to deal with those who wielded power. Within months, I was forging links with politicians. With my predecessor's support, I also began to direct the work more towards the Middle East, in the belief that one of the greatest challenges that faced us now was the potential for conflict between the West and the Islamic world. This book is about the attempts I have made since then to build bridges between East and West. This work is so difficult, but it is now my life. Despite my deteriorating health, I have no plans to give it up. In recent years, my focus has moved from Israel, the West Bank and the Gaza Strip to Iraq. It may be the most dangerous place in the world, but it has the most wonderful people.

Though I spend most of my time engaging with diplomats and politicians, I do everything in the power and to the glory of the Almighty. I will never forget my experience of his glory at St Mark's, Kennington, when I was a student at St Thomas' Hospital, or my encounter with Ruth Heflin in Jerusalem. But I needed so much to have the presence of the glory of God with me constantly as my work in the Middle East developed, and so it was a great joy to me when a friend persuaded me to visit the congregation led by Mahesh and Bonnie Chavda in Charlotte, North Carolina. There, at All Nations Church, I found again the presence of the glory of God, and from that day on the Chavdas' church became my church, and their people my people. They pray for me faithfully. They pray that the presence of the glory of God – the almost physical manifestation of the Almighty that radically challenges and changes the 'normal' world, which I see even in Baghdad – will be the thing that makes the impossible possible.

As my work has become ever more complex and difficult, it is only the presence of the glory of God that has enabled me to do what I have to do. With God, all things are possible. So, come with me on this seemingly impossible journey and maybe you, too, will see the glory of God making things possible.

CHAPTER 1

Declaration
of Intent

ONE DAY, I SHALL TELL the whole story of
my involvement in the Holy Land (or, as I
prefer to call it, the land of the Holy One).
For the purposes of this book, I am going to recount
two major developments in 2002 that I played a part
in, both of which gave me invaluable experience that I
was to use in Iraq in the years that followed.

For several years I had been going back and forth
to Jerusalem, working hard with my colleagues on a
number of grass-roots projects that brought Israelis and
Palestinians together. We had also been trying to bring
together Christians around the world. The Church –
not least, the Church of England – is still very divided
over the Holy Land. Sadly, most Christians either love
Israel and the Jews and disregard, or even despise, the
Palestinians (including Palestinian Christians) or they
love Palestinian Christians and hate Israel and the
Jews. Usually, they seek to justify their position from
scripture. I found this very disturbing – at the very

heart of Jesus' teaching is the command to love your enemy, and yet so many of his followers today seemed readier to take sides than to seek reconciliation. I had endeavoured to bring unity to the Church on this issue – for example, taking groups of British church leaders to Israel and the West Bank on behalf of the Anglo-Israel Association – and had had some success as people saw the pain and the need of both sides in the struggle; but in general I had failed.

Then came the year 2000, the so-called year of jubilee. Many millions of pilgrims were expected in the Holy Land, and many millions of dollars had been poured into repairing the infrastructure of both Israel and the West Bank. The most famous pilgrim of all was to be John Paul II. Hundreds of thousands flocked to see him, and Israeli television actually covered his whole tour live. It was an amazing time, and the Pope with great diplomacy managed to keep everyone happy, even the politicians. The image that remains in my mind most clearly is of his visit to the Western Wall. The plaza was empty as he slowly approached the ancient stones, accompanied by one other person: Michael Melchior, a government minister who was an Orthodox Jew and (as it happened) the Chief Rabbi of Norway. I didn't know it then, but Rabbi Melchior was soon to become one of my closest colleagues and friends.

Towards the end of that year, things started to go wrong politically. The fragile Oslo Accords were beginning to break down. President Bill Clinton had tried very hard at Camp David to forge an agreement on 'final status' negotiations between Yasser Arafat, the President of the Palestinian Authority, and Ehud Barak, the Prime Minister of Israel, but without success. The two sides told very different stories about what had actually happened. Subsequently, Israeli areas came under attack – in particular, rockets and mortar shells were fired into Gilo, a new town (some would see it as a settlement) on the outskirts of Jerusalem, from the adjacent Palestinian town of Beit Jala. Next, massive rioting erupted after Ariel Sharon (then leader of the opposition in the Knesset) visited the Temple Mount. Within days, what was to become known as the al-Aqsa Intifada had been declared. Violence was escalating rapidly, scores of people were dead and everything was falling apart. I would often cry to God with the words of the psalmist: 'How long, O Lord? How long?'

Hope evaporated – and, to make matters worse, the conflict seemed to be becoming increasingly religious in character. The very fact that this new *intifada*, or 'shaking off', had been called 'al-Aqsa', after one of the world's holiest Islamic shrines, seemed to suggest this. I continued travelling back and forth to Jerusalem, meeting with senior politicians, diplomats and religious leaders on both sides, searching for a way forward. Then, one day in 2001, over breakfast at the Mount Zion Hotel, everything changed. I was sitting with Gadi Golan, director of religious affairs in the Israeli Foreign Ministry, and he suggested that I should meet Rabbi Melchior, the man who had accompanied the Pope to the Western Wall. Now Deputy Foreign Minister, he was, Mr Golan said, a man who cared deeply about the role of religion in peacemaking. Like him, he had a vision to try to get all the religious leaders of the Holy Land to call for peace in this sacred place.

For the first time in a long while, I saw a chink of light. Maybe we could find peace again in the land of the Holy One. Maybe its religious leaders could play a positive role rather than a negative one. My meeting with Rabbi Melchior was very promising. We talked about the kinds of people we would need to involve and then discussed who should summon them all together. We decided it could not be either a Jew or a Muslim; it had to be a Christian. The Pope was too old and unwell for such an initiative, so we resolved that the person we had to approach was the Archbishop of Canterbury, George Carey, who had recently made a very successful visit to Israel and had also been to see Mr Arafat in Ramallah. Shimon Peres, then Israel's Foreign Minister, concurred that he would be the right person, and I was to be the one to ask him.

Dr Carey is a kind and wise man with whom I get on very well, and he agreed to our proposal without any hesitation. That was the easy part. Now we had to find a suitable place where we could invite the religious leaders to come together. I decided that Egypt would be best, as a country where Jews, Christians and Muslims could safely meet in the Middle East. Next, we needed to speak to the key religious and political players there to get their support. I was assisted in Egypt by three exceptional people: Mounir Hanna, then Bishop of Egypt in the Episcopal Church in the

Middle East; Dr Ali El Samman, a former diplomat who was now an adviser to the Grand Imam of al-Azhar, Sheikh Muhammad Sayed Tantawi; and the British ambassador to Egypt at the time, John Sawers. They devoted many hours to this endeavour and could not have been more helpful. Finally, we chose Alexandria as the venue, and specifically the exclusive Montazah Palace Hotel, which had its own extensive and very secure private grounds on the sea front. I made several visits to the city to make preparations and had many meetings with senior religious figures, from the Grand Imam to the head of the Coptic Church, Pope Shenouda III.

In Israel, the negotiations were intensive. We agreed that, if we wanted to be sure that this summit would be regarded as a success, it would have to issue a serious declaration. I wrote the first draft of this myself with my assistant, Tom Kay-Shuttleworth, and we would discuss it into the small hours with the various delegates on the planning committee we had formed. It took several weeks of this before they finally approved it. It was now nearly Christmas and I had to return home to Coventry for a week. The gathering had been scheduled for March 2002, but on Christmas Day Rabbi Melchior phoned me to say that it could not wait that long: the violence was escalating so sharply, and so little progress was being made on the peace process, that the declaration was needed as soon as possible. I told him he needed to speak to Dr Carey, which he did immediately. The following day, I travelled 160-odd miles down to Canterbury to see the

Archbishop. He had listened to Rabbi Melchior and, after asking my advice, decided to bring the summit forward to January.

Some of his staff were not exactly pleased by this – it meant major changes to his diary, including the cancellation of a trip overseas. Within a few days, I was back in Jerusalem, trying to finalize details. It was a mammoth task. There was also the issue of money – the summit was not going to be cheap and we needed the funding quickly. To find $200,000 in a few days was not easy, and I don't think I have ever prayed so hard for money. I approached a friend of mine, Lady Susie Sainsbury, a committed Christian who chairs the Anglo-Israel Association, and she came up with more than half of what we needed from one of her trusts. Other funds came from the Church of Norway and the World Conference of Religions for Peace, which were both to send observers.

I did further work on the ground in Jerusalem and the West Bank, spending hours with Yasser Arafat, representatives of the Israeli government and various religious leaders. While the Israeli team was led by Rabbi Melchior, the Palestinian Muslims were led by the equally inspirational Sheikh Talal Sidr, who was a minister in the Palestinian Authority. The Christians were to be led in Alexandria by the Latin Patriarch of Jerusalem, Michel Sabbah. Tom and I would talk with them into the night at the Mount Zion Hotel as we worked on the final draft of the declaration. We also shuttled back and forth to Cairo, where we spent hours with Dr El Samman going through the document word by word to ensure that it was acceptable to the Grand Imam of al-Azhar, who as the highest authority in Sunni Islam was to be co-chair with Dr Carey of the gathering in Alexandria. In addition, we had regular sessions with the British ambassador, John Sawers, the Israeli ambassador and representatives of the Egyptian government. All of these meetings were very positive. So far, so good.

Then, on 19 January 2002, I returned to London to brief Dr Carey before our scheduled departure for the Holy Land the next day. Things there were now very difficult. Furthermore, the Israelis had decided that no foreigners were allowed to see Mr Arafat (though by now I had realized that such bans usually didn't apply to me). On my way into Lambeth Palace, I met a senior member of the Archbishop's staff who politely informed me that we would not be going if he had anything to do with it. He didn't believe we would get access to either Mr Sharon (who was now Prime Minister) or Mr Arafat, let alone secure their support, and he thought I was just wasting Dr Carey's time. The two of us went in to see the Archbishop, and this man gave him his advice. Calmly and quietly, Dr Carey said that nonetheless we were going.

Early next day, Tom and I made our way to the VIP lounge at Heathrow to meet Dr Carey. His wife, Eileen, was accompanying him – like him, a quite exceptional person – as well as two of his staff. With me, unusually, at Dr Carey's insistence, was my wife, Caroline. I briefed the Archbishop during the flight and in due course we landed in Tel Aviv, where we were met by Britain's ambassador to Israel, Sherard Cowper-Coles. He had been very helpful to us and now he gave us a warm welcome. In Jerusalem, we were met by the consul-general, Geoffrey Adams, who was responsible for Britain's relations with the Palestinians. He, too, had been very supportive.

After dinner with him and his wife, we were driven in armour-plated cars to see Yasser Arafat in his compound, the Muqata, less than ten miles away in Ramallah. We arrived there surrounded by Palestinian security vehicles with sirens screeching; but, despite the tension outside, it was a very pleasant meeting. Mr Arafat could not have been more positive. He told Dr Carey how important the gathering in Alexandria would be, as religious leaders from Israel and Palestine came together for the first time to search for peace. Also present at this meeting in Ramallah were Ahmed Qurei (also known as Abu Ala) and Mahmoud Abbas (or Abu Mazen), who were both to serve as prime minister of the Palestinian Authority the following year, and Mr Arafat's chief negotiator, Saeb Erakat. (Early on, I had had some heated arguments with Mr Erakat, but later he was to become a good friend.) We returned to Jerusalem feeling encouraged, to wait to hear whether we would be able to see Ariel Sharon.

As the sun rose the next day, things were looking hopeful. It seemed we would be able to meet Mr Sharon that very morning, before a Cabinet meeting. Accompanied by Mr Cowper-Coles, Dr Carey and I made our way to the rather spartan prime ministerial office, where we were joined by Rabbi Melchior and his immediate boss, Shimon Peres, who, always very supportive, now endorsed without reservation the declaration we had drafted. Mr Sharon was a different matter. On his desk, he had a copy of the Hebrew Bible (as he did for all meetings with religious leaders) and he reminded the Archbishop of the words of Pope John Paul II: that to Christians this was the Holy Land, but to Jews it was the Promised Land. The message we got was: 'Don't mess with our land!' Nonetheless, it was remarkable that both Mr Sharon and Mr Arafat, two people who would not talk to each other, approved our draft declaration. It was this agreement that we wanted to seal and share with the world.

It was at Ben Gurion Airport, where we were due to catch a specially chartered plane to Alexandria, that the problems really started. There were some 45 people in our party in total, including the Archbishop (who had insisted on travelling with us rather than flying VIP, to show solidarity with the Palestinian dignitaries – who of course had no privileges at all). We had given everyone's name to the Israeli security services beforehand, and were also being accompanied on the flight by some agents from Mossad. However, while the Jews and Christians got through all the checks without difficulty, it was a very different matter for some of the Muslim delegates. The computers at passport control almost blew up! They could not allow these individuals onto an aircraft at Tel Aviv. For well over an hour we tried every argument and appeal we could think of to get them through. By now the whole party, archbishops, rabbis and all, was insisting that

THE VICAR OF BAGHDAD

if our Muslim colleagues could not board the plane, none of us would.

At long last, we were all allowed through. Mr Cowper-Coles, who was still with us, had rung Danny Ayalon, Mr Sharon's senior foreign-policy adviser, and some key people in Israeli intelligence, and this had done the trick. We were finally on our way to Alexandria. The plane landed very late, and then, surrounded by Egyptian police, we were driven to the Montazah Palace complex. My staff from Coventry Cathedral were already there and fortunately had removed from the bedrooms every painting that featured a naked woman, so that no offence would be caused to such senior religious leaders.

The summit began without further delay, at about 3pm. As Dr Carey opened the proceedings with a moment of silence, there was an air of great expectation in the room. We all knew we were on the verge of making history. The official language of the meeting was English, but there were interpreters on hand, provided by the Egyptian government, to translate to and from Hebrew and Arabic. The Israeli government had had the declaration we had written printed out on beautiful parchment paper, and I imagined that the signing was a mere formality before we got down to discussing our real business: how to put it into practice. To my horror, however, it became apparent that some of the Palestinian delegates would not sign it as it stood. The Christians had not really been involved in the weeks of preparation, and Patriarch Sabbah and the Anglican Bishop of Jerusalem and the Middle East, Riah Abu el-Assal, in particular believed that the declaration did not adequately reflect their concerns. In my experience, Christians in Palestine often seem to feel they have to be even more Palestinian than the Muslims, to show how committed they are to the cause.[1] To be honest, this (as well as the rivalries and tensions between the different denominations) can make them very difficult.

Had all our work been in vain? When George Carey wrote his autobiography, *Know the Truth*, after his retirement as Archbishop of Canterbury, he said that this meeting was the hardest he had ever chaired. I don't doubt it. The delegates separated to work through the issues, with Bishop Riah and Archbishop Boutrous Mu'alem sitting with the six Israeli delegates, as they were entitled to, in the hope that they could influence them. The sticking points were not theological but political, the principal issues being whether the statement should mention the Israeli occupation of the West Bank and Gaza and whether as it stood it implied that Palestinians were largely

---

1. Of the five Christian delegates, Patriarch Sabbah, Bishop Riah and the Melkite Archbishop of the Galilee, Boutrous Mu'alem, are all Palestinians holding Israeli citizenship. Archbishop Aristichos, who was representing the Greek Patriarch, is a Greek Cypriot, though he has lived in Jerusalem now for over 40 years. The late Archbishop Chinchinian, who was representing the Armenian Patriarch, was a Syrian living in Egypt.

responsible for the bloodshed. The Palestinians made it clear that they thought the Israelis were primarily to blame. If the declaration was to condemn violence, they insisted, it must condemn the violence that had been committed against their people. The issue of the right of Palestinian refugees to return to their land in what is now Israel also came into the dispute.

Much of the discussion was conducted in separate groups, but periodically we all came together and then there was a great deal of shouting on both sides. It was obvious that all the delegates alike felt strongly that they must not undermine their own politicians or betray the interests of their people. At first, no one was willing to move an inch – and in any negotiation when this happens it generates anger and frustration. I had to keep my opinions and emotions to myself – my role was to go back and forth between one group and the other to try to find a form of words acceptable to both. In the end, it was the Israeli rabbis who proved to be more prepared to give ground, though not on major issues such as the status of Jerusalem.[2] The only man on the Palestinian side who was ready to make compromises was a Muslim, Sheikh Talal. He had himself moved a considerable distance in his own life, from being one of the founders of Hamas to serving as

2. Apart from Rabbi Melchior, the Jewish delegates were Eliyahu Bakshi-Doron, the Sephardi Chief Rabbi; David Rosen, a former chief rabbi of Ireland who was now head of the American Jewish Committee's department of interreligious affairs; Menachem Froman, the Orthodox rabbi of the West Bank settlement of Tekoa, who has pioneered interfaith dialogue with leaders of the PLO and Hamas; and two influential members of the Chief Rabbinical Council, David Brodman and Yitzak Ralbag.

a minister in Yasser Arafat's administration.

Typically, only the most senior Muslim delegates
– Sheikh Talal and the chief justice of the Palestinian
shari'a courts, Sheikh Taysir al-Tamimi – actually took
part in the debate at all. The other two, the muftis of
Bethlehem and of the Palestinian armed forces, did
not say a word. (In fact, after the summit was over, the
latter went to live in Britain and, to my knowledge,
never returned to the West Bank.) As for me, when I
wasn't needed by the various delegates I sat with Dr
Carey and the Grand Imam, who were not involved in
the minutiae of the discussions. The latter had a long
conversation with the Sephardi Chief Rabbi, Eliyahu
Bakshi-Doron, which in itself was quite historic.

At midnight, Dr Carey retired to bed, after
instructing me that the problems must all be sorted
out by the morning. Into the small hours the delegates
argued in their separate groups, battling to find a
resolution. I moved constantly between the Palestinians
and the Israelis, but found them both so fixed in their
positions that I began to despair. How could we move
forward in the face of such intransigence? At 5am, I
went to bed myself. It had certainly been the most
difficult meeting I had yet taken part in, and I was
almost in tears as I went back to my room. I woke my
wife and we prayed, but it all seemed hopeless. Night
after night we had worked. We had all seemed to be
moving in the same direction, we had gone so far and
got so close, yet it looked as if now we were going to
lose everything. Probably for the first time ever, I asked
myself the question: Why were we failing? My past

experience of conflict resolution had taught me that people can change their minds very suddenly – but in the Middle East, it seemed, Western techniques simply did not work. I lay awake thinking about my calling to be a minister of the gospel. Was this really what it was about? I longed to be back in my old parish in London, where the people loved me and I loved them; but I knew deep down that that was no longer my calling. My true vocation was what I was doing now.

Three hours later, I got up to go and tell Dr Carey that we had not succeeded. When I spoke to Tom, however, he actually encouraged me. 'We mustn't give up,' he said. He had been with me from the beginning of this process, an outstanding assistant, and he had deep faith. He, too, knew that God had called us to this and he was not going to quit. That morning, we were joined once again by John Sawers. He is a wise man and he, too, was not going to let this historic endeavour founder.

After breakfast, the Archbishop of Canterbury called everyone together. He was very firm and very fair. He told us we had until lunchtime to deliver; otherwise, he was going to tell the world's media that the religious leaders of the region had failed to come to an agreement. We went on working in small groups. I was with Mr Sawers, going through those issues that were proving particularly problematic. A crucial advance was his suggestion: the insertion in the declaration of a call, as a necessary 'first step', for the implementation of the recent recommendations of two American envoys, George Mitchell and George

Tenet, who had looked for ways to build on the Oslo Accords. In particular, they had urged the Israelis to lift restrictions on the Palestinians in the West Bank and Gaza and to admit other Arab nations, such as the Syrians and the Saudis, into the negotiations.

By lunchtime, we were almost there. Dr Carey allowed us a little more time, and after another two hours we came to a satisfactory conclusion. It was now three o'clock. Now all we needed to do was to get the assent of Ariel Sharon and Yasser Arafat, since the religious leaders on both sides needed political support. A press conference had been arranged at another, more accessible hotel nearby for 5.30pm. We had just over two hours. Mr Sharon readily agreed with the compromises the Israeli delegation had made, but getting the approval of Mr Arafat was not so easy. His most senior aide, Nabil Abu Rudeinah, was adamant: the President always slept in the afternoon and could not be woken under any circumstances. Sheikh Talal took the phone from me and tried to talk him round. Finally, Nabil Abu Rudeinah agreed to wake the President on condition that I promised never to ask such a thing again. I promised. Mr Arafat was duly woken, and was happy to endorse the declaration.

At this juncture, one of the Palestinian Christians came to me and asked if we could add a reference to 'the end of occupation'. By now I was exhausted and I also knew that adding even one word would have brought the whole process to a halt, so I nodded as if to say yes and didn't change a thing.

This is the wording that was finally to be signed,

on 21 January 2002:

In the name of God who is Almighty, Merciful and Compassionate, we, who have gathered as religious leaders from the Muslim, Christian and Jewish communities, pray for true peace in Jerusalem and the Holy Land, and declare our commitment to ending the violence and bloodshed that denies the right of life and dignity.

According to our faith traditions, killing innocents in the name of God is a desecration of His Holy Name, and defames religion in the world. The violence in the Holy Land is an evil which must be opposed by all people of good faith. We seek to live together as neighbors respecting the integrity of each other's historical and religious inheritance. We call upon all to oppose incitement, hatred and misrepresentation of the other.

1. The Holy Land is holy to all three of our faiths. Therefore, followers of the divine religions must respect its sanctity, and bloodshed must not be allowed to pollute it. The sanctity and integrity of the holy places must be preserved, and freedom of religious worship must be ensured for all.

2. Palestinians and Israelis must respect the divinely ordained purposes of the Creator by whose grace they live in the same land that is called holy.

3. We call on the political leaders of both peoples to work for a just, secure and durable solution in the spirit of the words of the Almighty and the Prophets.

4. As a first step now, we call for a religiously sanctioned cease-fire, respected and observed on all sides, and for the implementation of the Mitchell and Tenet recommendations, including the lifting of restrictions and return to negotiations.

5. We seek to help create an atmosphere where present and future generations will co-exist with mutual respect and trust in the other. We call on all to refrain from incitement and demonization, and to educate our future generations accordingly.

6. As religious leaders, we pledge ourselves to continue a joint quest for a just peace that leads to reconciliation in Jerusalem and the Holy Land, for the common good of all our peoples.

7. We announce the establishment of a permanent joint committee to carry out the recommendations of this declaration, and to engage with our respective political leadership accordingly.

Now it had come to the point when we had to print out this definitive version, we found that the printer had stopped working. My PA, Sue Cutter, got it typed up in Arabic, Hebrew and English, and Tom taped it all together – one of the most important documents in religious history – and blew it up on the photocopier so there would be room for all the signatures. Finally, we took it in to the delegates and suddenly the anguish of the past three months gave way to elation. '*Al-hamdu li'llahi*' ('Thank God!' in Arabic) shouted the Palestinians. '*Baruch ha'shem!*' (the same in Hebrew) shouted the Israelis. They hugged and kissed each other, and then stood together to put their names to this statement that affirmed that killing innocent people was a desecration of the name of God – a point on which both Israelis and Palestinians very strongly agreed. The First Alexandria Declaration of the Religious Leaders of the Holy Land had been signed at last, and signed with joy.

I rang Lady Sainsbury and said simply: 'We've done it!' I knew that she and others had been praying for these secret discussions, and without those prayers I don't think we would ever have made it. Like most achievements of real worth, it had not been easy. For me, the pain it had involved had been almost physical. I have said as much as I can about how it was accomplished – I doubt that the whole story will ever be told. It was only a beginning, of course, but it *was* a beginning: for the first time ever, leaders of the three great faiths of the Holy Land had said with one voice that violence in the name of God had to stop. Moreover, they acknowledged that the declaration was only a beginning – they spoke of the need to continue to work together to see this initiative through.

The press conference was very positive: nobody spoke of the pain that had been involved in getting this far, and there was unity in our diversity. The following day, we all flew to Cairo on a chartered plane to meet President Hosni Mubarak and present him with the declaration. By the time the Israelis and Palestinians returned to Jerusalem, yet another bomb had gone off; but this time there was real empathy among all the delegates. They had started out as strangers to each other, but they had ended up as friends.

Back in Cairo, Caroline, Tom and I had lunch with the Careys and John Sawers before returning to London via Rome, where I stopped off to brief the British ambassador to the Holy See. As we left Egypt, Tom turned to me and said: 'I've just been part of what will probably be the most important event of my life and I'm only 24!' It was probably true – and without his organization and encouragement the whole thing would not have happened. In the Israeli and Arab press, the Alexandria Declaration was big news for days, but the Western media barely mentioned it. The major lesson we had learned was that often the most important steps we take are the most painful.

We set up a permanent committee for the implementation of the declaration, and at first this met almost every month – twice with Dr Carey present. After a year, we decided to hold a meeting at Lambeth Palace, a week before he was to step down as archbishop. There are very few people who would have even attempted such a crucial meeting a week before retirement! The day before we convened, a very important event took place at Coventry Cathedral, where the Coventry International Prize for Peace and Reconciliation was presented to the three protagonists of the Alexandria Process: Rabbi Michael Melchior, Patriarch Michel Sabbah and Sheikh Talal Sidr. It was a highly emotional occasion. There in the ruins of the old cathedral, on the 63rd anniversary of its destruction by German bombs, three key leaders of their people accepted this notable honour. For the sheikh, it was particularly significant. Here was one of the founders and former leaders of Hamas, a radical organization committed to the destruction of the state of Israel, receiving a prize for peace. Ken Taylor, at the end of his term as Lord Mayor of Coventry, described this day as the most moving and memorable of his year in office.

The next day, before our meeting at Lambeth Palace, something occurred that will stay in my memory forever. A Jewish businessman hosted a lunch in London for Rabbi Melchior, Sheikh Talal and me. There were many journalists present, and one of them, an Arab, shouted at the sheikh: 'How can you sit with this evil Zionist?' The sheikh paused and then, taking the rabbi's hand, he declared: 'This man is my brother and we will walk this long and difficult road of reconciliation together until we find peace.' 'What do you think you're doing?' someone called out. Sheikh Talal replied: 'I am pulling up thorns and planting flowers.' Suddenly, I realized that this was indeed the work God had called us to. A former advocate of violence was doing what the Prince of Peace calls us all to do. Whenever I am losing hope – which is often – it is this exchange I think of, and it enables me to keep going for another day.

Seven years after the signing of the Alexandria Declaration, the violence and bloodshed in Israel, the West Bank and Gaza continue. Nonetheless, I believe it has made an important difference. The process that produced it has given birth to a large number of other initiatives. Many grass-roots projects have been established by the delegates that involve both Israelis and Palestinians – arranging exchanges and encounters between schools, for example, and training up people to go and teach students of Orthodox Judaism and Islam about the other faith and its adherents. There is now an interreligious council that brings together the key Jewish, Christian and Muslim leaders. There is an Israeli and Palestinian Institute of Peace, with centres in Gaza, Jerusalem and, in the north of Israel, Kafr Kassem, where in 1956 Israeli border police had shot dead 49 Israeli Arabs, including 11 children. Furthermore, behind the scenes we are talking with some of the more radical Palestinian leaders who advocate or condone killing in the name of God.

New people have become involved. Sheikh Talal Sidr sadly died in August 2007, but in some ways his role has been filled by Sheikh Abdullah Nimr Darwish, who was the founder of the Islamist movement in Israel. He didn't come to Alexandria because he didn't think the summit would achieve anything – and he told me so in front of Yasser Arafat. Today, he is a key member of the permanent committee for the implementation of the Alexandria Declaration. He is a great man of peace.

So, we accomplished much. Even so, the work had only just begun.

CHAPTER 2

A Painful
Delivery

THIS IS THE MOST TRAUMATIC chapter of
this book to write. It tells the story of the
39-day siege of the Church of the Nativity
in Bethlehem, the birthplace of our Lord, a siege that
affected not only the people trapped in the church but
all the inhabitants of the city and the neighbouring
towns of Beit Jala and Beit Sahour. For most of that
time I was a witness to their sufferings, all day and
every day. By the end, I was exhausted physically,
emotionally and spiritually. I remember that I finally
went home in tears.

The story began for me on 2 April 2002. I was in
hospital in Coventry, being given steroids intravenously
after a relapse in my multiple sclerosis. I was in a private
room so I could have my five mobile phones switched
on, and suddenly one of them rang. The voice at the
other end of the line informed me that the *Ra'is* – the
President, in Arabic – wanted to speak to me. As soon
as Yasser Arafat came on the line, I could tell he was

distressed. 'They've taken our church!' he blurted out. 'We need you quickly!' As he explained what was happening, I realized I was already watching it live on the news. More than 200 Palestinians – a mixture of heavily armed gunmen, policemen and civilians – had sought refuge in the Church of the Nativity from the troops of the Israeli Defense Forces, which had invaded Bethlehem in strength in search of wanted militants. Now, along with some 60 priests, monks and nuns, they were surrounded by highly trained paratroopers backed up by tanks.

I said I was a little tied up at the moment but I would get there as soon as I could. Reluctantly, Mr Arafat accepted that assurance. Ten minutes later, my phone rang again. This time, it was the Deputy Foreign Minister of Israel, Rabbi Michael Melchior. Although he is a friend of mine, his manner was not quite as cordial as Mr Arafat's had been. 'I told you that if you left, something like this would happen. Get back here quickly!' he said. Only half in jest, I replied: 'So, it's all my fault, is it?' I told him I was in hospital, and I will never forget his response: 'Who do you work for?' For a moment, I was speechless. He knew I worked for God and he believed that, however poorly I felt, God would get me to Bethlehem soon.

I got a sense of the enormity of the crisis when the Archbishop of Canterbury, George Carey, called me. He was, however, just as concerned about me as about the situation at the church and didn't want me to discharge myself from hospital prematurely. So, I waited patiently for another day and finished my course of treatment while my project officer, Alex Chance, got us onto the earliest possible flight to Tel Aviv. He was an outstanding assistant and his help with my often hectic schedule was always invaluable.

When Alex and I arrived in Jerusalem, we began quickly to assess the situation. It was bad – probably the worst I had ever known it. A military operation called Defensive Shield was well under way throughout the West Bank and much of the territory was under siege, including the Muqata in Ramallah (where the men who had assassinated Rehavam Ze'evi, the Israeli Minister of Tourism, in Jerusalem in October 2001 were said to have taken refuge). At the Church of the Nativity, an Israeli sniper had already shot the bell-ringer dead, thinking he might be a suicide bomber. The people inside the church compound had little to eat or drink, and were ill equipped to negotiate with their besiegers or deal with their persistent demands and threats. There was an oppressive atmosphere of fear.

Our first task was to see Dr Emil Jarjoui, a wonderful paediatrician and the only Christian on the PLO executive. Alex and I went to his home in Jerusalem many times to discuss exhaustively what could be done. At the same time, we were going back and forth between the Palestinians and the Israelis as unofficial intermediaries, but it was impossible even to get them to agree on who should do the negotiating. The Israelis refused to deal directly with the gunmen inside the church, as the Palestinians wanted, because they regarded them as terrorists. It wasn't long before the world's media discovered that I was involved, and requests for interviews began to pour in.

During this period, I made frequent excursions into the West Bank to visit Bethlehem, just a few miles across the border from Jerusalem. What I saw when I passed through the checkpoint was quite unbelievable. The only vehicles on the roads were either Israeli tanks, armoured personnel carriers and military trucks or the cars and vans of international television. Along the main streets, Israeli armour had bulldozed the lamp posts and smashed the frontages of houses, shops and hotels. The reek of burnt-out cars and buildings enveloped the whole city in the stench of senseless destruction. I had been in Bethlehem, Beit Jala and Beit Sahour many times, but had never seen them in such a state before. In recent months, the situation had deteriorated drastically. Beit Jala, a predominantly Christian town, is barely 500 yards across the valley from the new Jewish town of Gilo, and Palestinian fighters had been forcing their way into houses that overlooked it to send a constant stream of rockets and mortar shells into that unfortunate place. As expected, the Israelis had responded by sending Apache helicopters to destroy the homes from which the missiles were fired. Once again, Christians were caught in the middle. Later, I learned that the militants involved were among the leaders of the group that then took refuge in the Church of the Nativity. The havoc they caused was to have dreadful consequences.

The negotiations about negotiations continued, and I spent my days talking to politicians and

Christian, Muslim and Jewish leaders. I also gave scores of interviews to the international media at the request of the British consulate in Jerusalem, which was concerned by the exaggerations being broadcast by both the Palestinians and the Israelis. Geoffrey Adams, the consul-general, was a fine man who was greatly respected by Dr Carey, and he proved to be an excellent person to work with. With the help of a local member of my Coventry staff, Hanna Ishaq, I was also devoting an increasing amount of time and money to helping the people of Bethlehem and the two neighbouring towns to obtain food and medicine. Whenever we took supplies in, we would at once be surrounded by children desperate for something to eat. It was becoming obvious that the crisis was affecting not just the people inside the Church of the Nativity but all the inhabitants of Bethlehem, Beit Jala and Beit Sahour as well.

One afternoon, I was contacted by an English woman living in Bethlehem. She had heard that a local man called Edmond Nasser, who had recently been to Jordan to have open-heart surgery, was in dire need. He lived on the edge of Manger Square, in the centre of the city, which was now completely cut off. Out of curiosity, I asked how she had got hold of me and she explained that the British consulate (knowing of my medical training) had told her to contact me. I took that as a divine directive that I had to try to help this man. Accordingly, I rang the local Israeli commander, with whom I had quickly become good friends. Shmueli Hamburger was a colonel in the reservists, a jovial and generally very obliging older man who worked in the Ministry of Religious Affairs with oversight of the Christian communities of Israel and the occupied territories. Now, everything in Bethlehem went through him. I told him I had to go into the city to help someone who was seriously ill, but he insisted that it was far too dangerous – there was too much shooting. It was obvious I was not going to get in through the front door.

I got word that Mr Nasser's condition was deteriorating. Clearly, we had to get to him as a matter of urgency. Hanna told me of a back route into Bethlehem: into Beit Jala by car and then on foot over some barren, broken ground where surveillance would be minimal. He drove us at speed to Beit Jala and then, with my medical bag in my hand, I clambered over the rocks with Alex at my side. Even then there was still another two miles to go, so we shouted for a car. It was wishful thinking – there was a curfew and the streets were completely empty – and yet within seconds a man came running towards us. He said his name was Mustafa, and it turned out that he had a vehicle, covered in TV network signs but with Israeli plates. I knew it was almost certainly stolen, but there was no time to worry about ethics.

When we told him where we needed to go, Mustafa laughed and said there was no way he could get us there. So, we asked him to take us back to Beit Jala, to the King Hussein Hospital, and on the way I rang Shmueli. He was amazed that we had managed to get so far, and promised to meet us at the hospital in his armoured car. Now he was willing to escort us into Bethlehem, and so it was not long before we reached the very heart of that beleaguered city. One of the most sacred places in the world, it was now a theatre of war. There were tanks everywhere; searchlights pierced the darkening sky, and from a crane hung a huge loudspeaker blasting out noise in a psychological assault on the gunmen trapped inside the church.

Finally, we arrived at the home of Edmond Nasser. Mustafa waited outside in his car while Alex and I ran in, not knowing what we would find. Mr Nasser was in a bad way. The incision from his operation was badly infected and showing signs of septicaemia, and it didn't help that he was clearly malnourished. He could not believe that someone had simply shown up with the very medication he so desperately needed. As a Christian, he was overjoyed that God had sent a priest to his aid. But I am not only a priest, and at times like this my medical training takes over. Once more an operating department practitioner, I swabbed his wound.

We gave him the provisions we had brought and talked with him for a while, and then we had to go. Shmueli warned us to drive slowly and follow his vehicle closely as we made our way through the stricken city. So we did – until suddenly, without a word of warning or explanation, Mustafa hit the accelerator. Driving like a madman, he sped away from our escort and recklessly turned into a side road. The ring of my mobile phone cut through our shock. It was Shmueli, angry and very alarmed. I asked

Mustafa what he thought he was doing, but he didn't reply. Shmueli ordered us to proceed directly to a nearby military base. 'We could be in big trouble now,' Alex commented drily, as perfectly composed as ever. When we arrived at the base, however, the colonel leapt out of his armoured car and, running towards us, threw his arms around me. When I asked him why his mood had suddenly changed, his answer appalled us. Just after he had rung me, someone had thrown a small bomb at Shmueli's vehicle which had landed just behind it. If we had still been following him, we would have all been killed. Mustafa never gave us an explanation for what he did, and I never saw him again. I have often wondered since whether he was, in fact, an angel – one with a Muslim name and a stolen Israeli car! Now at Christmas when I sing about angels in Bethlehem, I cannot help but think of him.

The next morning, we carried on with our laborious negotiations about negotiations. Mr Adams told me I should work with Alastair Crooke, who (he informed me) had been seconded from the Foreign Office to the European Union as a security adviser to Javier Solana, in effect the EU's foreign minister. I made contact with him and over the next month we spent most of our time working with him. He was a quiet man in his fifties, obviously very intelligent. He had a deep understanding of the Palestinians and could always see their point of view. We got on very well.

The Israelis made it clear they didn't want any religious leaders to take part in the actual negotiations, but when eventually they and Yasser Arafat's office came up with their respective lists of people they wished to be involved, both of them included my name. I went back to the Israelis and asked them how come I was on their list. They laughed and told me I wasn't a religious leader. I didn't know what to make of that.

By now two men had been killed inside the church by Israeli snipers, who believed they were armed. We were told that their bodies were being kept in the grotto where Jesus is said to have been born. They were already decomposing, and there were ever more insistent threats from the besieged gunmen that, if we didn't remove them soon, they would bury them in the church. This raised the very real risk that this Christian shrine could become the burial place for Muslim martyrs. I spent many hours with the Greek Orthodox Patriarchate trying to work out how we could retrieve the bodies and get them back to their families. The Israelis did not want anyone to go into the church, and apparently the militants did not want anyone to come out. It would take another ten days before this problem was resolved.

It was now 14 April. The siege was almost two weeks old but still no real negotiations had begun. It was on this day that the Israeli Prime Minister, Ariel Sharon, informed the world of his government's position: the Palestinian fighters in the church could either surrender and be tried by an Israeli military court or go into permanent exile. Yasser Arafat responded with his own announcement: There would be no trial in Israel and no exile. The dispute between the two men was very public – though, as he himself was under siege in the Muqata, Mr Arafat was not actually in any position to influence events.

Talks were still not under way six days later when we were told that there was no food or water left in the church. We were now meeting with other people who had been named as negotiators. Alastair Crooke was by now with me and Alex all the time, and it was decided that we would be based mainly with the Palestinian team in Beit Jala, at the home of the Palestinian Minister of Tourism, Mitri Abu Aita. With Shmueli's co-operation, Hanna was able to drive the three of us into Bethlehem. Day after day, we were told that face-to-face talks were about to begin, but they never did. The Israelis did not seem to be in any hurry.

At last, on 23 April, over three weeks after the siege of the church began, negotiations got under way. The Israeli team was composed entirely of military personnel, led by a very professional and pragmatic lieutenant-colonel called Lior; the Palestinian team was led by Salah Tamari, a former PLO commander (and a very good friend of mine) who was now a member of the Palestinian Legislative Assembly. At this point I thought the crisis would soon be over, but that was far too optimistic. The talks took place in the evenings under heavy security in the Peace Center in Manger Square. They were conducted in English, though only Palestinians and Israelis were present, and Lt-Col Lior followed a strict agenda. A crucial participant was a highly respected Christian lawyer called Tony Salman, who was a member of Bethlehem's municipal council.

He was actually one of those who had taken refuge in the church, and was the only one that both the gunmen and the Israelis would allow to go in and out. He was our sole contact with the militants, and our principal source of information about what was going on inside the compound.

During the day – day after day – Alastair, Alex and I sat with the Palestinians at the minister's house, discussing negotiating tactics with them in a room full of tension and blue with cigarette smoke. The minister's wife made us wonderful food to maintain our energy levels as the three of us spent hours talking to the Israelis on the phone or simply waiting. Salah would often be heard shouting angrily down the line to Yasser Arafat, who, like Ariel Sharon, was not willing to make any compromises. Alex and I were working with Alastair to try to find solutions to the impasse – I was to learn a great deal from him about hostage negotiations. By now it had become obvious to us both that he was not your average diplomat, and I could well believe the rumours that he worked not for the Foreign Office but for the Secret Intelligence Service, MI6 and had been engaged in covert operations from Colombia to Afghanistan.

Perhaps this explained why he wouldn't deal with the media. In fact, there was always a large number of reporters outside the gates of Mitri Abu Aita's house. I had got to know many of them well, but now we were actually engaged in negotiations we had to try to keep as low a profile as possible. This was easier said than done. The minister had a 12-year-old son who had made friends with many of the reporters and we often saw him holding their cameras or microphones. Sometimes he even brought them into the house, and then all the talking had to stop.

On 24 April, on only the second day of formal negotiations, we finally saw some progress – despite the fact that two more Palestinians inside the church compound had been hit by Israeli snipers. (One of them, a policeman, was to die later.) By now we had realized that the situation in the church was in effect a double siege: many of the people inside the compound were trapped there by fear as much of the gunmen as of the Israelis outside. (The foreign religious had said they were staying as 'voluntary hostages', to show solidarity with the Palestinians and to try to deter any more bloodshed.) However, the militants now agreed that nine teenagers could leave the church and could bring the two badly decayed bodies out with them. The following day they emerged, carrying their burden in makeshift coffins. They were questioned by the Israelis, and one of them was detained on the suspicion that he had been involved in planting explosives in Jerusalem. The two dead men were identified as policemen.

Things were becoming increasingly desperate in Bethlehem, Beit Jala and Beit Sahour. Shmueli kept us informed of the more urgent needs he was aware of, and one day he came and told us that the Ethiopians hadn't had any food for three weeks. I hadn't even been aware that there were Ethiopian monks in Bethlehem. It turned out that they lived very close to Manger Square, which meant we couldn't get to them

ourselves, so I sent Hanna out to find as much food as
he could and we entrusted it – bags and bags of it – to
Shmueli. When he returned a couple of hours later,
I asked him: 'Well? Were they happy with the food?'
His answer astonished me. 'No! You forgot to include
any lemons!' To this day, I have never again forgotten
the lemons.

Alex and Hanna and I spent hours every day just
driving around obtaining and delivering food and
medicine. I was becoming concerned that we were
running out of funds – the needs were so great and our
resources were so small. The Archbishop of Canterbury
regularly rang me to ask about the humanitarian
situation, and in time he sent a very considerable
amount of money. It was certainly very welcome.

The atmosphere in the house of Mitri Abu Aita
grew more and more tense. Salah was still shouting
down the phone to Mr Arafat, and the bitter fog of
cigarette smoke grew ever thicker. The Israelis were
adamant that those men in the church whom they
regarded as terrorists would have to be deported, and
one of my principal concerns was to find somewhere
they could go. My primary contact was a man in
Italian intelligence called Aldo. One possibility we
were investigating was to send some of the militants
to the Arsenal of Peace in Turin, a former weapons
factory that was now a Roman Catholic monastery and
peace centre. I also spent many hours with the three
patriarchs of Jerusalem – the Greek, the Armenian and
the Latin – who shared control of the Church of the
Nativity; and in addition I was seeing both the senior

Franciscan in Jerusalem, the Custos of the Holy Land, and the papal nuncio, Archbishop Pietro Sambi.

On 27 April, Alastair went with some of the Palestinian team to see Yasser Arafat in Ramallah, but I wasn't surprised to learn when they got back that they had achieved nothing. The outcome of meetings with Mr Arafat often depended on his mood. On this occasion he had clearly not been having a good day, and while they tried to talk with him he just continued signing a pile of paperwork in his customary red ink.

We were getting reports that the situation in the church compound was now very serious indeed and people had been reduced to eating the boiled leaves of the lemon trees that grew in the courtyard. Salah kept offering to go in to try to get the civilians out in return for provisions for those who remained. Time and again, however, the leaders of the various groups of gunmen in the church refused to accept this offer. The Israelis were insisting that any food that was taken in must be supplied by them, and the militants knew that they would make political capital out of their supposed magnanimity. It was all part of the game the Israelis were playing.

On 29 April, the siege of Mr Arafat's bunker in Ramallah was finally lifted when the four men accused of killing Rehavam Ze'evi were tried and sentenced by a hastily convened Palestinian military tribunal. Briefly we believed that a similar deal might be possible in Bethlehem, but the Israelis soon made it clear that that was out of the question. They had withdrawn their forces surrounding the Muqata only under intense pressure from the Americans and regarded that as something of a humiliation, and they felt they could not afford to show any leniency in Bethlehem. In fact, that same day another Palestinian was shot by an Israeli sniper. Nidal Abayat had been one of the leaders in the church. The Israelis regarded him as a serious threat and he was on their 'most wanted' list – it was he and some of his relatives who had been responsible for firing rockets and mortar shells into Gilo from Beit Jala. Now he was dead.

The next day, 24 more people were allowed to leave the church – but the provisions that were meant to be sent in in exchange for them were never delivered. Lt-Col Lior admitted that the Israelis were now concentrating not on negotiating an end to the siege but on 'increasing the pressure' on those inside the compound, and he was no longer sure that he had the authority to send in food. By now we were all very tired and becoming very frustrated with the lack of any real progress. After so many strenuous days and sleepless nights, we seemed to be going nowhere. Then we were informed by Lt-Col Lior that the Israelis were going to allow Salah and Alastair into the church to get the names of everyone inside. Up until this point, we didn't even know how many people were in there, let alone who they all were. The Israelis were just as eager to find out as we were, though they still made out that they were doing us a favour.

An agent of Shin Bet, Israel's domestic security agency, then told Salah and Alastair that this was to be the last part they would play in proceedings, as

the Palestinian and Israeli negotiating teams were
both to be disbanded. This was a real surprise to
me. Nothing of any great significance had yet been
accomplished. What was going to happen now? We
knew that President George Bush had been under
immense pressure to intervene. The behaviour of its
close ally Israel was damaging America's relations with
the Arabs. The *intifada* was already compromising the
'war against terror', and any further complications
could undermine the attempt to build a consensus for
action against Saddam Hussein. Now, it seemed, the
Americans were going to get involved in Bethlehem.
Exhausted and exasperated, Alastair and I returned
with Hanna and Alex to Jerusalem, with no idea of
what the future held. We went to a café for lunch,
and then managed a couple of hours' sleep before
we were informed that there would be a meeting
that afternoon at the King David Hotel (famous as
the location in 1946 of the Zionist bombing of the
British military headquarters in mandatory Palestine).
When we arrived, we found that the Americans were
represented by two CIA men, the Israelis by some
agents of Shin Bet and the Palestinians by Muhammad
Rashid, Mr Arafat's Iraqi-born Kurdish adviser.

The four of us were told exactly what was
required, of us and of others. Of course we were happy
to co-operate in any way we could, but I couldn't see
that the new plan was very different from anything
we had already suggested. What *was* clear, however,
was that the Americans expected things to happen
and to happen right away. The plan was quite bold,

requiring that some of the gunmen, whom the Israelis and the international community alike regarded as terrorists, should be put on trial at the International Court of Justice at The Hague. This was not at all what Mr Arafat wanted, though Mr Rashid agreed to it and he was one of the most powerful members of the Palestinian National Authority. (After this meeting Mr Rashid disappeared and to this day I have not seen him again, though I heard once that he was in Egypt. I suspect he felt that in consenting to this plan he had destroyed his credibility with ordinary Palestinians.)

The final outcome, however, was rather different. It was decided that the 13 militants who were on Israel's 'most wanted' list were simply to be sent into permanent exile abroad and another 26 would be removed to Gaza, to stand trial in Palestinian courts for seizing the church and for other alleged crimes against Israel. This all sounded fairly simple, but we still didn't know for certain where the 13 could go. We had been talking to the Italians, but at that stage we had thought that only seven men were going to be expelled.

On 2 May, a group of peace activists from the International Solidarity Movement somehow managed to get into the church with some food – I have no idea how – to add yet another complication to an already complex situation. Nonetheless, by the following day nearly all the arrangements had been made and Alastair, Alex, Hanna and I were instructed to go to Beit Jala to meet a new Palestinian negotiating team, led this time by one of the President's relatives, a man with a face badly scarred by burns, who also was called

Arafat. He had presided over the trial of Mr Ze'evi's killers in Ramallah and, as his court had managed to try, convict and sentence them all in a single morning, we knew he was a man of decision. Nonetheless, he and his colleagues had been trapped inside the Muqata for a month and they had only a very limited idea of what had been going on in Bethlehem.

The CIA then showed up, four big men who spoke perfect Arabic and drove identical SUVs. Neither Alastair nor I were fluent in Arabic, so we asked Hanna to eavesdrop on them for us, which he did very well. (Afterwards, he told us that these had been the best days of his life!) Next, we had to get hold of a floor plan of the church, to find somewhere where the 13 'senior terrorists' (as the Israelis called them) could be locked up for a couple of weeks, once the siege had been lifted, while arrangements were made for their expulsion. It did not prove easy. I asked the Mayor of Bethlehem whether he had the plans, but he told me that as the church was much older than the municipality, he did not. Eventually, however, I did locate them. It turned out that a friend of mine in Jerusalem, Dr Petra Heldt, knew the person who had them – as it happened, at Oxford University.

The end seemed to be in sight, when I received a phone call from the same English woman who had alerted me to Edmond Nasser's plight. Now she was speaking on behalf of the peace activists inside the church. Apparently, they had decided that they would leave the building only on two conditions: that Yasser Arafat told them to and that they knew what was going to happen to them. It was now three in the afternoon, the hour when Mr Arafat always took a nap. I phoned Nabil Abu Rudeinah and asked him if he could possibly wake the *Ra'is* with this new, urgent request. He reminded me that earlier in the year I had had Mr Arafat woken with regard to the Alexandria Declaration and told me I simply could not expect to do it again. So, the activists stayed where they were.

There was a further obstacle. Now the Italians knew how many men were going to be expelled, they not only were adamant that they would not take 13 of them, they insisted they had never been asked to take even one. We had been talking to Rome about this critical issue for weeks, yet everything now was denied. It was a stunning blow. All we could do was to carry on frantically looking for a country that was willing to accept these most unwanted men. At least we now had the help of the EU's special envoy to the Middle East, the Spanish diplomat Miguel Ángel Moratinos. Alex and I had met him at the Spanish consulate in Jerusalem and we knew him well and counted him as a friend. He had also worked with Alastair before.

By 9 May, we seemed at last to have a workable plan. The 13 men were to be flown to Cyprus and held there in detention in the Flamingo Hotel until the members of the EU had decided where they should finally go. Quickly, all the arrangements were made, right down to the metal detectors to scan everyone as they came out of the church. Midnight came and all we were waiting for was the coaches the CIA had promised to provide, to take the 13 to Ben Gurion Airport and the other 26 militants to Gaza. As I watched from a rooftop overlooking Manger Square, I listened to the many reporters talking to camera around me. As usual, none of them got their facts right. Among them was Michael Georgy, an Egyptian-American Christian who worked for Reuters. He had always been very persistent in trying to extract information from me about the negotiations – though without success – and I must admit I had become rather fond of him. Tonight, however, the principal thing on his mind was not the end of the siege but the BBC's Middle East correspondent Orla Guerin. He confessed to me that he wanted to marry her. I told him he was stupid: she was too sensible for him.

The promised coaches did not materialize – we never found out why – and at 7am I finally gave up and went back to Mitri Abu Aita's house. Another night wasted! I wanted to get back to Jerusalem, but Hanna fell asleep so deeply that nobody could wake him, though everyone tried. The following night, we returned to Manger Square to wait for the coaches, and this time they appeared. In the early hours of Saturday 11 May, the 39 surviving gunmen who had taken refuge in the Church of the Nativity finally emerged, weak but defiant. As agreed, two-thirds of them were taken to Gaza while the 13 the Israelis regarded as the most dangerous, accompanied by Alastair, were put on an RAF Hercules transport plane to Cyprus. As I watched them go, I cried with relief. The whole thing had been so traumatic and so protracted – and in those days I wasn't used to that. I little imagined how much harder things could be – and, in Iraq, were to be. I was utterly exhausted. I made my way to the airport and after five gruelling weeks was very glad when I landed in England.

Eleven days later, EU negotiators announced that of the 13 exiles being held in Cyprus, three would be permitted to live in Italy, three in Spain, two in Greece, two in Ireland, one in Portugal and one in Belgium. The last, who had been Yasser Arafat's chief of intelligence in Bethlehem and was viewed by the Israelis as the worst of all, was eventually accepted by Mauritania six months later. The 26 militants who had been removed to Gaza were set free as soon as they arrived there and never did stand trial.

I didn't see Michael Georgy again until 2003, when I bumped into him outside the Palestine Hotel in Baghdad after the liberation of Iraq. He told me he'd been looking everywhere for me. I asked him why and he said, 'I want you to marry us.' I asked him who he was marrying and he said: 'Orla, of course!' I didn't believe him, so I gave him my phone number and told him to get her to call me. Eventually, she rang me to assure me that it was true, and would I officiate at their wedding. A few months later, I married them in Ireland. This was the one good thing that resulted from the siege of the Church of the Nativity: that the worst journalist in the world got to marry the best. And yes, I did say that at the wedding!

CHAPTER 3

....

From
Darkness to
Darkness

I HAVE TOLD THE STORY of how I first became
involved in Iraq in my earlier book, *Iraq: Searching
for Hope* (Continuum, 2007), whose second edition
took the narrative up to 2006. Those who have read
that book may want to skip this chapter. Here I will tell
the tale again, more briefly – though with the benefit
of a little hindsight.

In the autumn of 1998, when I took over from
Canon Paul Oestreicher as director of international
ministry in Coventry, I had to decide where in the
world our work of reconciliation was most urgently
needed. It was obvious to me that our top priority had
to be engaging with the Islamic world. One area of
particular concern was Israel/Palestine, where I had
been a regular visitor. Another was a country I had
never been to: Iraq. We were beginning to hear of the
terrible impact on its people of the Gulf War of 1991

and the sanctions that were afterwards imposed by the United Nations to try to prevent Saddam Hussein from rebuilding his military machine. America, Britain and France had also enforced no-fly zones in the north and south of the country to protect its Kurdish and Shia populations from attack by his forces. Finally, in December 1998, President Bill Clinton ordered major air strikes on Baghdad.

I tried several times to get a visa to enter Iraq, but I was always told that our help was not needed. Finally, in March 1999, I assembled my team in the cathedral and together we prayed that we would get permission to go there without more delay. The next day, a fax arrived from Tariq Aziz, the Deputy Prime Minister of Iraq, asking me to meet him in his office in Baghdad the following week. As Archbishop William Temple once said: When you pray, coincidences happen and when you don't, they don't. I flew first to Amman in Jordan, and from there I was driven across the desert to the Iraqi capital. It was a hard, 13-hour slog that was soon to be a regular part of my life. The highway inland from the border was very good, but in Baghdad everything was extremely shabby. I was taken to my hotel, al-Rashid, where I met the secret policeman who was to be my companion throughout my stay. My room looked dirty – in fact, I couldn't imagine that a hotel bedroom could look worse. Ten years later, there *is* a hotel whose rooms are even worse – it's al-Rashid.

I soon began to learn about the nature of Iraq. There was no prospect of doing what I wanted to do, or even seeing what I wanted to see. I was taken to meet a wide variety of political and religious leaders, Sunni, Shia and Christian. With me at all times were my minders from Iraqi intelligence, the Mukhabarat. Everyone I met said the same thing: the country was being crippled by the sanctions and by the depleted uranium that had been used so liberally by the Allies in their munitions in the 1991 war. Everyone was frightened of my minders, though it was a long time before I realized this – but that didn't make what they were all telling me any less true. I was taken to a hospital where ward after ward was full of children dying either from malnutrition or from malignancies caused by uranium dust. It was a very disturbing experience, as it was meant to be.

That evening, I went to see the cigar-smoking Mr Aziz – the first of many such meetings. He made a very significant request: he wanted me to return soon with some bishops and other church leaders. I assured him I would do my best. The next day, I found I was both relieved and sad to leave Iraq. I was aware of the tension and fear that oppressed this country, but in a strange way I felt I was falling in love with its people, even though at that stage I really knew nothing about them. On the interminable drive back to Jordan, all I could think of was those words from Psalm 137:

By the rivers of Babylon we sat and wept...

I returned just seven weeks later, by the same exhausting route, with four others: Colin Bennetts, my bishop in Coventry; Peter Price, then Bishop of

Kingston, my old diocese; Clive Handford, then Bishop of Cyprus and the Gulf, whose diocese included Iraq; and Patrick Sookhdeo, the international director of Barnabas Fund, which at the time was helping me and my colleagues with our work for reconciliation among Muslims in the Middle East. Once again, this visit was very productive. Most of our meetings were with people I had met before, but there were two people new to me who would make a big impact on my life. One was Margaret Hassan, the local director of the humanitarian organization Care International. Five years later, she would be the first good friend of mine to be taken hostage in the chaos that engulfed the country, though she was married to an Iraqi and had herself become a Muslim. I and my team would be involved in the harrowing effort to rescue her, but without success. The other was Georges Sada, the president of the Protestant Churches of Iraq, a passionate Christian who had been an air vice-marshal in the Iraqi air force before he retired in 1986. He quickly became my indispensable right-hand man, and was to remain so until 2005, when he was headhunted by the Americans to run Iraq's new Ministry of Defence.

Mr Aziz was delighted that I had returned so quickly with my trio of bishops. Now he had a new request: he wanted us to take a delegation of Iraqi religious leaders not only to Britain but also to America. I told him I thought America would be impossible, but Mr Aziz had the answer: Ask Billy Graham! He can do it, he said – and he was right.

With Dr Graham's strong support, it did indeed happen, in September 1999. The three delegates chosen by the Iraqi government – one Shia, one Sunni, one Christian – were all very senior people. Two of them I had met before: Ayatollah Hussein al-Sadr – like all ayatollahs, a direct descendant of Imam Ali, Muhammad's son-in-law and the founder of Shia Islam – and Mar Raphael I Bidawid, the Chaldean Catholic Patriarch. The third, however, was new to me. Sheikh Dr Abdel Latif Humayem was in effect Saddam's personal imam; he had made the pilgrimage to Mecca on his behalf and was said to have written out a copy of the Qur'an in the dictator's blood. He was also the principal preacher on Iraqi television every Friday, for which the CIA report on him described him as 'the Billy Graham of Baghdad'.

For five days, these three dignitaries had to wait in Amman while the American embassy there refused to give them visas. Finally they were allowed into America, to meet Dr Graham and the former president Jimmy Carter (and to see the Niagara Falls), but only after they had been photographed and fingerprinted like criminals. In Britain, on the other hand, they were received as VIPs. In Coventry, Bishop Colin proved to be a wonderful host. The programme was very intensive, but two meetings were especially memorable. The first was a warm and frank discussion with the Archbishop of Canterbury, George Carey. I had no idea that a few years later he would be a colleague of mine, and a very close friend.

The second took place at the Royal Institute of

International Affairs at Chatham House. Towards the end of the evening, some people from the Al-Khoi Foundation stood up. They unrolled a huge scroll with over two hundred faces pictured on it and asked the ayatollah to tell everyone who these people were. He knew there were informers in the room, and so the only answer he would give was a quotation from the Qur'an. In the end, one of his questioners told the audience himself that they were members of the ayatollah's own family who had been killed by Saddam's regime or had otherwise disappeared. At the back of the auditorium stood a man who did not speak to the ayatollah but simply looked at him with tears running down his cheeks. It was only years later that I discovered that he was one of Ayatollah al-Sadr's closest friends, though they hadn't seen each other since he had fled to London in 1979. In Britain he was known as Mow Baker, a neurologist; but after the war he went back to his own country and resumed his old name, Mowaffak al-Rubaie. He was then soon appointed to the new, 25-strong Iraqi Governing Council, and later was given a five-year contract as National Security Adviser by the country's American administrator, Paul Bremer. Today, he is one of my closest friends and advisers.

These few days forged some crucial friendships, and sealed my relationship with the Christian, Shia and Sunni communities of Iraq. The patriarch sadly passed away only two months after the liberation of his country, but ten years on I still count Ayatollah al-Sadr and Sheikh Dr Abdel Latif among my closest allies as they work with me to try to heal the sectarian division in their nation. The ayatollah is a man of great holiness and wisdom, whom I consult over everything I do in Iraq. The sheikh is a delightful man. Remarkably, they have developed a strong affection and respect for each other.

One other man I have to mention is Fadel Alfatlawi, a postgraduate student in Coventry who acted as our interpreter throughout this visit by his countrymen. When he returned to Iraq after the fall of Saddam, I invited him to become a member of my team. Just over a year later, he would succeed Georges Sada as secretary general of the new Iraqi Institute of Peace.

After this, I visited Iraq several times a year. I always went to see Mr Aziz, at his insistence, and often took him a bottle of his favourite brown sauce – for which the British media accused me of 'playing with the Devil'. I was forever on Iraqi television condemning the sanctions. With Georges beside me, I was involved in many projects concerned with both opening channels of communication and relieving suffering – not least, helping to set up Iraq's first-ever bone marrow transplant centre and bringing its medical team to Britain for training. I met most of Saddam's ministers many times (though I never met Saddam himself). I continued to deepen my relationships with the various religious leaders I knew. My only concern was to bring relief and promote reconciliation – though it left an unpleasant taste when I was obliged to have dinner with Saddam's two odious sons and they thanked me for all I was doing.

I was sitting in my study in Coventry on 11 September 2001 preparing to leave for Iraq the next day when news broke of the attacks on the World Trade Center and the Pentagon. It was obvious that nothing was ever going to be the same again. It was also obvious that I was not going to get to Baghdad the next day. I did make it a few days later, however, and the first thing Tariq Aziz said – or shouted – when I met him was, '*Abuna* ['Father'] Andrew, tell them we had nothing to do with it! We are revolutionaries, not terrorists.' I replied without thinking: 'Your Excellency, it doesn't matter whether you are terrorists or revolutionaries, they are still coming to get you.' And it was true. Suddenly, the CIA wanted to talk to me about Saddam's weapons of mass destruction – I was no longer just a nuisance. I assured them that those weapons existed. I still insist that I know this for a fact. They were never found because they were moved out of the country before the UN's weapons inspectors arrived. (In his 2006 book *Saddam's Secrets*, Georges was more explicit: there were chemical weapons in Iraq as late as the summer of 2002, which were then spirited away to Syria.)

When I went to Baghdad in October 2002, I knew it would be the last time before it came under inevitable attack. I had started out trying to work for reconciliation between Iraq and the West and I had failed, as I was acutely aware – but I no longer believed that this was what the Iraqis needed. Now I felt strongly that the Ba'thist regime had to be removed. I was no longer opposed to the very idea of war. Everywhere, people would tell me quietly that someone had to set them free from Saddam's tyranny. They knew there was nothing they could do themselves. Late on my last night in Baghdad, I escaped my minders and went for a walk with Georges. I asked him: 'How can you keep going when everything seems so dreadful?' He quoted some words from the prophet Habakkuk:

> *Though the fig tree does not bud*
> *and there are no grapes on the vines,*
> *though the olive crop fails*
> *and the fields produce no food,*
> *though there are no sheep in the pen*
> *and no cattle in the stalls,*
> *yet I will rejoice in the LORD,*
> *I will be joyful in God my Saviour.*

In the years that followed, these have been words that strengthened me and enabled me to persevere.

I was in Cambridge, writing a short book on a fellowship from Clare College, when the war began. Saddam was given 48 hours to leave Iraq, and when the deadline expired on 20 March cruise missiles and bombs began to rain down on the city and the people I loved. I could see no alternative, but the emotional pain I felt was still intense. The collapse of the Ba'thist regime was very quick, however, and it wasn't long before we were watching Saddam's Minister of Information, Muhammad Sayed al-Sahaf (whom I knew and liked), insisting on television, 'I triple guarantee you, there are no American soldiers in Baghdad' even as an Abrams tank was visible over his shoulder entering the city. Hours later, the whole world saw the huge statue of the dictator in al-Ferdos ('Paradise') Square being hauled down by the Americans and stamped on by Iraqis. (Today, the top half of that statue is in Dr Mowaffak's living room.)

Now that people in Iraq could talk freely at last, I was appalled to discover that in all the years I had been visiting their country even those close to me had been too afraid to tell me of the true horror they lived under. It was only now, for example, that Georges admitted that he had been imprisoned for nine months in 1991 for refusing to kill prisoners of war. My driver, Nashwan, told me that his own father, a general, had had an eye gouged out after he refused to obey a brutal order. Both he and Georges were reckoned to have got off lightly.

I lost no time in going to see Ayatollah al-Sadr at his home in Baghdad, and there I learned from his disciples how cruelly the regime had tortured this old man. Others told me of their own suffering. One man had been buried for several days inside a coffin. Another had been a day late in returning from a trip to Syria. The Mukhabarat took him to his home, where they were already holding his family prisoner. First they raped his wife in front of him, and then they picked his three-year-old son up by his ankles and smashed his head against the wall. Finally, they shot the rest of his family dead before they left. That was the nature of Saddam's regime.

It soon became clear that the tragedy of Iraq was not over, however. The Coalition made some very serious errors. Its troops had stood by while all the hospitals, museums, universities and libraries, and all the ministries except the Ministry of Oil, were comprehensively looted – but this was not its most catastrophic mistake. First, it failed to secure the country's borders. The first time I drove from Amman to Baghdad after the war, the border control consisted of one smiling American soldier chewing gum, and the only question he asked was 'Where are you guys from?' Soon, Iraq was being infiltrated both by militant Shia from Syria and Iran and by al-Qa'ida and other Sunni radicals. I myself encountered three young British Asians on the border with Jordan who told me they had come 'to fight the Coalition'.

I had already warned the British and American governments of the likelihood of sectarian conflict and I had urged them to engage with Iraq's religious and tribal leaders as a matter of urgency, but they thought that as a priest I was just beating my own drum. I still have the dismissive letter I received from the Foreign Office at the start of 2003 telling me that religious issues would have to wait until the water and electricity supplies had been sorted out. Today, as I write this in October 2008, water and electricity are still scarce. The ignorance of the Americans especially was sometimes quite disturbing. They had no real understanding of Iraqi society and assured me that it was essentially secular. They even proposed to set up a national religious council in Baghdad after the war whose 12 members would include six women – and not one cleric! The British were more knowledgeable, but they were simply ignored. Neither government seemed to me to have any real plan for the peace.

I have read Rajiv Chandrasekaran's book about the American administration of Iraq after the war, *Imperial Life in the Emerald City*, and I have to say that the picture it paints is very accurate. The Coalition Provisional Authority was a well-meaning shambles. There were so many hundreds of experts – but they were experts in setting up systems that work in America. And not everyone was even that: the man who was given the job of reviving the Baghdad stock exchange was a junior soldier who had never worked in finance! Paul Bremer, who took over the reins from the ex-general Jay Garner and his very short-lived Office of Reconstruction and Humanitarian Aid, was a splendid man but he knew absolutely nothing about the Arab world. His previous experience, as ambassador to the Netherlands and 'ambassador-at-large for counterterrorism' under Ronald Reagan, did not qualify him for overseeing one of the most complex societies in the world. It was reportedly his unilateral decision to dismiss every last man in the Iraqi army and police. Clearly, some people had to go, but the result of sacking everyone was the anger and anarchy that engulfed the whole country. Suddenly, hundreds of thousands of men trained to fight (and still in possession of their weapons) had no job, no income, no status and every reason to revolt. In the CPA headquarters in Saddam's huge Republican

Palace, the Ministry of Justice was located underneath a flight of stairs.

A new darkness descended on the land. The very day after Saddam's statue was pulled down, my friend Abdel Majid al-Khoi was hacked to death by a mob in the holy city of Najaf. Only a few days before, at a conference on religion and violence at Windsor Castle, I had sat for dinner with him and Prince Philip. This young ayatollah, still only 40 years old, had told me that the Americans wanted him to return to Iraq from his exile as soon as possible to help with the task of reconstruction, and he asked me to go with him. I said I thought it was still too soon to go, but he went and now he was dead. No one knows who ordered his killing, though an Iraqi judge later issued a warrant for the arrest of another Shia cleric, Muqtada al-Sadr, the fiery young nephew of Ayatollah al-Sadr whose militia, the Mehdi Army, was to become such a challenge to the Coalition.

The murder of Ayatollah al-Khoi can be blamed on the struggle for power between rival Shia factions, but that was not the only source of conflict. I have already mentioned the rapid infiltration of Iraq by militant Shia and Sunna, who hated the West and also hated each other. Neighbouring countries such as Syria and Iran got involved, partly to hurt America and partly because they felt threatened by the prospect of a democracy next door to them. Many of the insurgents were former supporters of Saddam who had lost money, prestige and power as a result of his fall. Others were simply taking advantage of the chaos to settle old scores or to turn to crime. There were people who had naively imagined that a free Iraq would become like one of the Gulf states overnight and were furious that it hadn't. In the few weeks after the war when I could still walk in the streets of Baghdad, I once found myself faced by a vast crowd shouting both 'Death to Saddam!' and 'Death to America!' Further anger would be provoked later in 2004 by the shocking abuses in Abu Ghraib and the bloody assault on Falluja (which took place during Ramadan), and by incidents – fortunately rare, but still dreadful – such as the massacre by US Marines at Haditha in 2005. And, finally, there were tens of thousands of young men without jobs who were willing simply to hire out their services as fighters.

Violent death soon became a feature of everyday life in Baghdad. The International, or 'Green', Zone was now surrounded by blast-proof barricades and coils of razor wire. The hotels outside it, in what came to be known as the Red Zone, were more like prisons – except that prisons do not usually come under rocket attack. Two atrocities in particular in August 2003 announced Iraq's descent into bloody chaos. A huge car bomb outside the Jordanian embassy killed 14 people and injured 40 others. Twelve days later, the country's first suicide bomber detonated a colossal explosion that tore apart the UN headquarters in the old Canal Hotel. The head of the UN mission, Sergio Vieira de Mello, another friend of mine, was among the 23 dead. Someone had finally got revenge for all the years of sanctions.

Since then, I have lost count of the friends and colleagues who have been killed. Samir, my new driver, and one of my project officers had a narrow escape when a 1,000lb car bomb went off outside the Palace while I was preaching at chapel inside. The heat was so intense that car doors were welded shut and people were burnt to death inside their vehicles. On many occasions, I myself have come very close to being shot or blown up. Hundreds of religious leaders, hundreds of politicians, have died. Nobody ever even tried to keep count of how many ordinary Iraqis were being slaughtered. There was a brief lull in the bloodshed when Saddam was captured at the end of 2003, but it didn't last. Many times over the next four years I would write in the regular 'spiritual updates' I send to my supporters: 'Every time I think the violence cannot get any worse, it does.'

As soon as the war had ended, I had been invited by the American State Department to become involved in the reconstruction of Iraq. At the very beginning I was dealing with Britain's 'special representative', John Sawers, my old friend from Alexandria, and our most senior soldier in Iraq, Major General Tim Cross. The latter had gained solid experience in Kosovo four years before – but it was he who suggested that I wait for a week or two before returning to Baghdad, 'when the situation will be under control'. Britain's 'head of mission' in Baghdad was Christopher Segar, a seasoned diplomat fluent in Arabic who quickly became a crucial ally. It was with and through him that our real search for peace began. He regularly met the various religious leaders I was engaging with, and he secured funding from the Foreign Office for our work. Today he is one of the trustees of my foundation. Paul Bremer was also very supportive, as was his British deputy, Sir Jeremy Greenstock. Day after day, Georges and I did the rounds of the key players, British, American and Iraqi. Everyone was interested in Ayatollah al-Sadr's idea for an Institute of Religious Tolerance, though Prince Hassan of Jordan, a friend of Lord Carey whose family had once ruled Iraq, told me that 'tolerance' was not enough – what was needed was mutual respect. Of course, he was right.

Sheikh Dr Abdel Latif had fled the country, but we finally tracked him down in Amman and from exile he did all he could to help us. Among the Sunna, his name alone was useful. My first meeting with Sheikh Dr Abdel Qadir al-Ani in Baghdad was going very badly, for example – he even accused me of working for the CIA – until I thought to mention that Sheikh Dr Abdel Latif was my friend. By the time our meeting ended, I had a firm commitment from him to work with us for peace. Other meetings proved equally tricky, but many of these had positive outcomes.

On 24 February 2004, after months of negotiation, we succeeded in bringing together many of the country's more influential religious leaders at the Babylon Hotel. Ayatollah al-Sadr and Sheikh Dr Abdel Qadir sat side by side at the head of the table – two of Baghdad's most eminent Muslims, meeting for the first time. Most of the country's faiths and sects were represented, though the Christian archbishops only turned up the following day to sign it – they felt very vulnerable in the new Iraq, and were afraid of being caught in the crossfire between the Shia and the Sunna. The Baghdad Religious Accord was based on the Alexandria Declaration (though we could never admit that). It affirmed that 'killing innocents in the name of God is a desecration of the laws of heaven', condemned sectarianism and committed its signatories 'to doing all in [their] power to ensure the ending of all acts of violence and bloodshed that deny the right to life, freedom and dignity'. In the end, it was signed by 39 religious leaders. There was a sense of triumph – it was a historic achievement, though it was only a start.

Four months later, the Dokan Religious Accord was signed by leaders in the Kurdish-dominated north of Iraq. The only difference in the wording was that, out of deference to the religious minority the Yazidi, it did not say that acts of corruption, violence and destruction 'are the work of the Devil'.

We had so much hope in those early days. We really thought we could make a difference. We worked hard, day and night, to implement the accords, and in particular to establish the Iraqi Centre for Dialogue – everyone had agreed that 'dialogue' must be in the title – Reconciliation and Peace. We set up six working parties to address the different aspects of our task:

- women, religion and democracy
- youth and young people
- the media

- religious freedom and human rights
- interreligious dialogue
- conflict prevention and resolution

Dr Mowaffak became the first chair of the ICDRP (soon to be renamed the Iraqi Institute of Peace), and for its headquarters in Baghdad we used a wonderful house on the banks of the Tigris that belonged to his wife. It soon became known simply as 'the Centre'. It was in al-Khadamiya, which is very much a Shia neighbourhood, and yet in those days everyone felt able to come there – though at its opening I counted 39 guards with sub-machine guns in the grounds. Sadly, however, our optimism was shattered one day when a relative of Saddam was brought to us so that we could turn him in. I rang the American embassy to ask them to collect him, and the Iraqi prime minister's office to let them know what was happening. Eventually, four US Navy Seals arrived and discreetly took him away – and 45 minutes later the Centre was surrounded by over a hundred plain-clothes police from the new Ministry of Interior, who beat me and threatened to shoot me, ransacked the house and stole our computers and over $20,000 in cash. It was a lesson in how divided and untrustworthy the new Iraqi government was. The next day, the British embassy asked me to move inside the Green Zone for my own safety.

Thereafter, we got used to these two extremes, of elation and despair. Whichever state you were in at the moment, you knew that the other was not far away. The progressive new temporary constitution was published in March 2004 on International Women's Day, and I shall never forget the sight of women dancing and singing and weeping on the streets of Baghdad. Yet it was less than a week before that a concerted series of attacks by al-Qa'ida had slaughtered at least 178 Shia worshippers, and injured at least 500 more, on their holy day of Ashura. The handover of sovereignty from the CPA to the Iraqi Interim Government on 28 June was marked by another spike of violence. As the date approached for the country's first democratic election, for a transitional assembly, the insurgents threatened to kill anyone who cast a vote; and yet on 30 January 2005 nearly 8.5 million people did so, and for a while the country was full of pride. Almost a year later, when the election for Iraq's new, permanent parliament, the Council of Representatives, took place, over 12 million people voted, a turnout of almost 80 per cent. All the while, however, the killing continued, and in fact it got worse.

One particular area in which we experienced both joy and grief – though, sadly, far more often the latter – was in negotiating for the release of hostages, which increasingly occupied my time after April 2004. Kidnapping had become an epidemic in the new Iraq. Most of the people responsible were petty criminals out to make some quick money, and the vast majority of the people they abducted were middle-class Iraqis or their children. However, if they managed to get a foreigner they would usually sell them on to terrorists, and then it was a different matter. British and Americans commanded much the highest prices – and were the most reported in the Western media, which generally ignored (for example) the poor Filippino truck drivers who were seized and in the end brutally murdered, often on camera. Through the IIP, I and my team became involved in many of these cases, and over time we acquired a lot of expertise. Often, the negotiations were very complex, uncertain and protracted, and they were always very fraught. Some of the Iraqis in my team were killed.

When I was appointed as director of international ministry at Coventry Cathedral in 1998, it was supposed to be for a term of five years. I finally left in July 2005, to continue the work that Ruth Heflin had foreseen for me, seeking 'the peace of Jerusalem and the Middle East'. I had already set up my own foundation with Lord Carey, and most of the key people who had worked for me while I was at the International Centre for Reconciliation in Coventry – Fadel and Samir in Baghdad, Hanna in Jerusalem – continued to work for me in my new capacity.

CHAPTER 4

A Measure
of Progress

T THE END OF AUGUST 2008, I was sitting
in a room in Beirut with four of Iraq's most
senior religious leaders when one of them
remarked that 'nothing had happened in 2006 and
2007'. None of us asked him what he meant. We all
knew. They had been such difficult years. We had
continued with our work, but as the fight for peace
continued, so did the kidnapping and the killing.
We had hoped for change, but it seemed so slow in
coming. The carnage just went on and on and on.
In just one day in November 2006, for example, 215
people were killed in Sadr City, the poor Shia suburb
of Baghdad, by mortar fire and car bombs. I wrote
then: 'In [2005,] I could still speak about specific acts
of violence and individual tragedies, but now the
slaughter is so unremitting it is almost impossible to
write about anything particular.'

It became impossible for the Iraqi Institute of
Peace to operate from its original base in al-Khadamiya.

This overwhelmingly Shia neighbourhood of Baghdad was under constant attack from the predominantly Sunni neighbourhood of al-Adhamiya across the river Tigris, and of course it was far too dangerous for the IIP's non-Shia clients to be seen there. In spite of all its difficulties, however, the IIP is still functioning today, with funding from the United States Institute of Peace. I have been trying to remove myself from its leadership, as is only right, but in fact my involvement has only increased. Fadel Alfatlawi has had to leave Iraq because of the huge price on his head, and he has been replaced as the IIP's secretary general by Essam al-Saadi. A former lawyer, like Samir, Essam also works for Iraq's National Security Adviser, Dr Mowaffak al-Rubaie, as his head of media relations. He is a Shia in his late thirties, highly dependable, very well connected on all sides and able to make things happen. Like me, he now lives in the Green Zone and since 2006 we have met every evening to talk things through. He has been present at all the Foundation for Relief and Reconciliation in the Middle East (FRRME) international summits (for which he also handles the media), and he and Samir and I have become known as 'the Triangle'. I had so many people in my team in Iraq at one stage, but now it often seems as if there are just the three of us.

Samir Raheem al-Soodani, who was originally my driver after the war, is now the Iraq director of the FRRME and the man I most rely on. He translates for me nowadays, as Professor Sadoon al-Zubaydi, Saddam Hussein's interpreter who subsequently worked with me, has gone to live in Jordan. Everyone we work with knows Samir and trusts him, and he, too, is someone who can make things happen. (I divide the world into people who can make things happen and people who can't. I reckon that only 4 per cent of humankind come into the first category, and these are the people I work with.) It is no longer safe for Samir's wife and daughter to stay in Baghdad and so, with the help of the Pentagon, they have won 'special parole status' in America. Samir himself has permission to live there when he is not in Iraq, but that is not very often and so he sees them very rarely.

All of us have faced serious death threats. I have had to flee Iraq on several occasions – most recently in July 2007, when pictures of me were posted up around Baghdad with the caption 'Wanted dead or alive'. They announced that if I did not leave the country, the hostages I was trying to recover would be killed (so the threat probably didn't come from al-Qa'ida). The British embassy ordered me to go and the next day I flew secretly to Bahrain. Even in England, in rural Hampshire, my wife and children had to move out of our home for a while because they were thought to be at risk. Caroline told me it was the first time she had been afraid because of my job – though I don't think the boys were bothered. After a month in Britain, I returned to Iraq. My colleagues had continued our work for peace without me, but I had St George's Church in Baghdad and the chapel in Saddam's old Republican Palace (now the American embassy) to look after as well. I have to admit that, although I have contemplated the fact that one day I may be killed in Iraq, or abducted, the thought has never once troubled me.

I have been very fortunate in the men who guard me – they have been outstanding. Originally, our security was provided by men of the Controlled Risk Group, at a (hugely discounted) rate of £750 a day. One day in 2006, I was sitting in my trailer in the Green Zone when there was a knock at the door. It was Paul Wood, a former Parachute Regiment officer who was now managing operations in Iraq for Kroll Security International, with whom we had worked closely on several hostage cases. He asked me how much we were paying for our protection and offered to halve the price. When CRG said it would match this, Paul said that Kroll would look after me and Samir for nothing. Since that day, his men have cared for me as if I were one of the family. Kroll was subsequently taken over by the Canadian company GardaWorld, which today takes care of all my needs in Baghdad, including my accommodation, my food and even my laundry. In May 2007, it was presented with the FRRME's first Prize for Peace in the Middle East in recognition of the phenomenal service it has given us.

In 2006, the Iraqi government was proving to be divided and ineffectual. Continuing wrangling over the new constitution was jamming the legislative programme, with disputes in particular over the decentralization of power to new autonomous 'regions' and the distribution of oil and gas revenues. Crucial bills were not being passed. The Council of Representatives (that is, the parliament) that was inaugurated in March soon began to lose faith in the Council of Ministers, who seemed unable to deliver on anything that really mattered to the country. Some people might say that these were the inevitable teething troubles of a new democracy, but Iraq could not afford such problems while the escalating violence was shutting down every basic service from electricity to education.

The government of Ibrahim Ja'fari fell at the beginning of May. I used to have regular meetings with Dr Ja'fari and I got on very well with him – he is a nice man, and a good one, though he was a weak prime minister. There was no obvious man to take his place, but eventually the big Shia coalition that had put Dr Ja'fari into power chose Nuri al-Maliki, the leader of the Da'wa Party. At first I didn't think he would have enough authority to survive, but I turned out to be wrong. He is a strong supporter of our work for reconciliation – he knows how difficult it is but realizes that it is the only way forward. I always enjoy my meetings with him.

Meanwhile, al-Qa'ida had become more active and effective in Iraq. In the early years after the war, its mostly foreign fighters had actually played quite a small role in the conflict, but it had the most recognizable terrorist 'brand' in the world and had (wrongly) been linked with Saddam in the build-up to the invasion, and so it is not surprising that its presence among the insurgents had a high profile in the Western media. There was great jubilation in the Pentagon when al-Qa'ida's 'emir' in Iraq, the one-legged Jordanian Abu

Musab al-Zarqawi, was killed in an air strike in June 2006 – but in fact its role in the conflict only grew bigger after that. Most of its fighters in Iraq today are Iraqis, and their impulse seems to be to attack anyone who does not share their extreme Sunni ideology. They see their country as the front line in their war against America, and want to prove to the world that the Americans are defeated – though in fact most of their victims have been their compatriots.

The struggle towards peace and reconciliation continued, but progress was painfully slow. Since the beginning of 2005, our primary objective had been to organize a major summit that we hoped would produce a statement similar to the Alexandria Declaration, agreed and signed by the key leaders of all the faiths represented in Iraq. Samir and I and the young American Peter Maki, who was then my director of operations, sat through endless meetings with politicians and religious leaders, inching our way towards this goal.

Then, one day in June 2006, I was informed by Jerry Jones, my friend and ally in the Pentagon, that the Department of Defense had decided to pay for the whole series of summits we were trying to arrange. This was a very significant breakthrough. The British Foreign Office had undertaken to fund our work for a year after the end of the war, and after the year was up that funding ceased. The American military had never invested in anything like this before, but now we had their support – and they are, without question, the biggest power in Iraq. Some people can only see the Pentagon as the enemy of peace, and cannot understand how we could accept its money and work so closely with its people. The fact is, however, that in Iraq the US Army has become our most important partner in the search for peace. Every day, I see the way its soldiers (sometimes literally) lay down their lives for this country. I see their strength and courage, and their commitment. It is difficult for some people to accept this, but the truth is that the greatest peacemakers in the world today are in the armed forces. Furthermore, in Iraq the US Army detailed its military chaplains to work with me.

The man behind these decisions was Gordon England, who in 2005 had succeeded Paul Wolfowitz as Deputy Secretary of Defense after the latter had moved on to head the World Bank. Mr England is a delightful man, and quite devout. Today, he is very much involved with our work. I always go to see him when I am at the Pentagon and he always listens attentively. Another useful ally there is the retired general Mick Kicklighter, a remarkable man of God who was a regular member of my Anglican congregation in the Palace back in 2004. He has never made any bones about the fact that he regards 'this Iraq business' as the Lord's work – and now he is the inspector general of the DoD.

In the autumn of 2006, we began to make concrete plans for the first of the meetings of what was to become known as the Iraq Inter-Religious Congress, or II-RC. At first we intended that this should take place in Britain, and I and my colleagues at the FRRME spent days making the arrangements and discussing the issues with the Foreign Office. The cost of security was a major concern. We had planned to meet in Surrey, in the south of England, but the police told us it would cost in the region of £1 million to ensure our safety. The Foreign Office told me I had three days to find the money, and obviously didn't think it was possible. I did find it, not in three days but one. When I informed the people at the FO, they told me the summit still couldn't take place in Surrey. I think they were always intending to say no: they support what we are doing, but they didn't want to see such a high-risk group of people in Britain.

Frustrated, we started afresh. We wanted to find a venue outside Iraq for many reasons: Baghdad was dangerous and many people were very reluctant to go there – the daily slaughter was just unremitting. It was unpleasant in other ways: even in its best hotel there was often no water in the taps. We looked at the possibility of meeting in Italy (where I had good relations with one of the intelligence services, after helping to secure the release of several Italian hostages in Iraq). We also considered Malta, because a friend of mine worked in its high commission in London, and the island offered some obvious advantages. However, neither government would give us permission, and in the end we decided that Baghdad was the only option.

The negotiations took many, many weeks. Often I would work into the small hours, only to be woken at six by a barrage of rockets. Before the summit itself, we went to Amman in April 2007 for a 'pre-conference' with some of the key Sunni leaders who would be attending. My American friends Bill and Connie Wilson, who are our principal 'prayer partners', came over from Jerusalem to pray for us in their room, and Colonel Mike Hoyt, the most senior of the American chaplains in Iraq, also accompanied us. For some reason, he spoke eloquently to the delegates about the concept of 'the separation of church and state'; but they couldn't really grasp it. To their minds, it was a nonsense: the two are indivisible.

I was constantly being told by Sheikh Dr Abdel Latif Humayem that we were still waiting for the most important delegates to arrive from Syria. Eventually they turned up and I sat down to talk to their leader, an Iraqi in his forties. I know who this man is, but I cannot identify him. He came across as an educated and cultured man and was well dressed, in Western clothes, but he proved to be the nastiest person I have ever met – and I have met some nasty people. It was a very difficult meeting, and at times I felt very angry. I believe Sheikh Dr Abdel Latif hoped that I could engage with this man, but it was soon evident that he had come only to threaten me. He told me at great length how both Britain and America were going to be attacked in retaliation for what they were doing in Iraq. He made a comment I will never forget, though at the time I did not understand what he meant: 'Those who cure you will kill you.'

That night, I wrote in a 'spiritual update' to supporters of my foundation, 'I met the Devil today.' A few days later, when I happened to see a senior official from the Foreign Office, I told him some of what this man had said, but I did not pass on that one, cryptic sentence: 'Those who cure you will kill you.' Within a few months, at the end of June, a plot to set off two car bombs in the West End of London was discovered, apparently in the nick of time. A day later, two men tried to explode a car full of propane-gas cylinders at Glasgow International Airport. In all, eight Muslim people were arrested in connection with these crimes. Five of them were doctors and two more were reported to be medical students.

On 3 July, I was sitting in al-Rashid, drinking tea with one of my very few British friends in Iraq, Debbie Haynes, and I told her about my meeting with the Devil and what he had said. I knew she was a journalist, but I didn't really think anything of it. The next day, 'Those who cure you will kill you' was the main headline on the front page of the London *Times*. That was the end of my low profile in Iraq. I gave 78 interviews to the media that day – they virtually had to form a queue.

It was at al-Rashid that we had finally held the first meeting of the II-RC the previous month, from 11 to 13 June. There was little electricity and no air conditioning, though the temperature rarely dropped below 45°C, and there was the constant threat of attack by rockets and bombs. At the time, I recorded my thoughts in these words:

Two-and-a-half years of non-stop work for two-and-a-half days of meeting. We spent well over $2

*million in preparation and spent months sitting
with some of the most difficult people imaginable.
In the past few weeks, [my team in Britain],
Samir and I have literally worked day and night
organizing this event. I have worked hard for
years, but nothing has ever been like this. In the
last day, [we] have been hardly able to talk. I
found one of my staff today asleep on the floor. This
peacemaking business is not easy...*

*Doing the event in Iraq has been far more
complicated than anywhere else. The security is
immense – we have helicopters, tanks and ground
troops even though it will be in the [Green] Zone.
The good thing is that the [US] Army is taking this
very, very seriously and risking nothing. I just hope
and pray that the delegates will all arrive safely.
The whole future of Iraq is at stake.*

In fact, this conference was the largest interfaith
gathering of religious leaders ever to take place in
Iraq. Some 70 religious and tribal leaders attended,
from all across the country, including Basra, Falluja
and Saddam's home town, Tikrit. The Kurds and
Christians were represented, too. Dr Mowaffak was
present, and several members of parliament, including
the Minister for Human Rights, Wijdan Michael Salim,
a Chaldean Catholic who is one of the outstanding
people in the government. (She and her whole family
have become very good friends of mine. The eldest of
her three teenage sons, Osama, came to Britain in 2008
with some of the young people from St George's.)

The wording of the accord they signed (in the presence of the ambassadors of America, Britain, Denmark and Italy) was similar to the Baghdad Religious Accord of 2004, though it wasn't consciously modelled on it, but there was one crucial difference: for the first time, Iraq's Sunni as well as Shia religious leaders denounced al-Qa'ida by name. This was also the first broad-based religious accord to recognize the constitution and to call on the Iraqi government to engage at a senior level with religious and tribal leaders. It also declared that the proliferation of unauthorized weapons was an offence. The delegates expressed a desire to continue to meet regularly to look at ways to reduce the violence, and they set up a number of working parties that would address specific issues, such as 'religion and culture' (fostering good relations between the different faiths and finding common ground on matters of morality and behaviour) and 'reconstruction' (rebuilding everything from mosques to sewers). It had the personal endorsement of the Prime Minister, Nuri al-Maliki, who sent his religious affairs adviser Sayed Dr Fadel al-Shara to sign it on his behalf and promised funding from the government. We understood, too, that Grand Ayatollah Ali al-Sistani – the single most authoritative figure in Iraq – was particularly supportive of the condemnation of the proliferation of weapons.

One thing I was very particular about was that we should bring together the various strands of peacemaking in Iraq, including not only the Baghdad and Dokan Religious Accords and the work of the IIP

With Pope John Paul II in 1992. My vicar at the time was rather taken aback that his curate received so many summonses to the Vatican.

Presenting a replica of Coventry's Cross of Nails to the late Raphael I Bidawid in the ruins of the old cathedral in 1999. Also in the picture are two men who were to become crucial allies in the cause of peace in Iraq: the wise and holy Ayatollah Hussein al-Sadr and the delightful Sheikh Dr Abdel Latif Humayem.

Archbishop Aristichos signing the Alexandria Declaration in 2002, watched by the Grand Imam of al-Azhar (seated) and two great men of peace: the late Sheikh Talal Sidr (standing, left) and Rabbi Michael Melchior (standing, right). In between them is Sheikh Tantawi's interfaith adviser.

Hanna Ishaq, my man in Jerusalem, who has worked with me longer than anyone. This picture was taken in Tel Aviv.

Visiting Yasser Arafat in the Muqata in 2003. The outcome of meetings with him often depended on his mood.

Talking to an American soldier in Baghdad. The statue of Saddam Hussein is one of four huge bronzes of him that used to adorn his Republican Palace.

Standing in al-Khadamiya in the short period after the liberation of Baghdad when it was still safe to venture outside the Green Zone. And we thought it was dangerous then…

A typical view in the Green Zone two years later. By this time, all our movements were controlled by concrete and plastic – as in the passes round our necks. Immediately behind me is Fadel Alfatlawi.

When Saddam's Palace became the headquarters of the Coalition Provisional Authority, his throne room was used as the chapel and whoever was leading the service would sit on his gold-plated throne. Here I am relaxing with two friends from the US Army.

Attending a gathering of Muslim religious leaders from Israel and Palestine in Cairo in 2005, to follow up the Alexandria Declaration. On my right is the chief justice of the Palestinian *shari'a* courts, Sheikh Taysir al-Tamimi.

With the then British Prime Minister, Tony Blair, and my great friend and co-worker for peace Lord Carey, early in 2007.

With Paul Bremer, ex-'king' of Iraq, at a dinner given in my honour at the Pentagon in 2007.

With General David Petraeus in 2007. On my left stands Samir; on the general's right stands Colonel Mike Hoyt and, beyond him, Peter Maki and another general. Unlike this picture, the US military is very focused!

With Ibrahim Ja'fari outside his prime ministerial residence, before his fall from power in May 2007.

With the
current Prime
Minister of Iraq,
Nuri al-Maliki.
Also pictured
are (left to right)
Peter Maki,
Colonel Hoyt,
Dr Mowaffak
al-Rubaie and
Samir.

Iraqi Shia and Sunni leaders meeting with the Grand Imam of al-Azhar (right) in Cairo early in 2007.

Enjoying the
hospitality of
my dear friend
Ayatollah
al-Sadr in No-
vember 2007.
On his right
stands Samir,
and next to
him the Danish
pastor Niels
Eriksen.

With my close friend and ally Dr Mowaffak (second from right), conversing with the Armenian Orthodox Archbishop of Baghdad, Avak Asadorian, in Copenhagen.

Listening intently in Copenhagen: left to right, a Kurdish sheikh, Sheikh Dr Abdel Latif, Sheikh Abdel Halimjawad Kadhum al-Zuhairi, Mrs Samia Aziz Mohamed and Yonadam Kana, the leader of the Assyrian Christian democrats.

With the former British prime minister Sir John Major and our respective wives (Caroline is on the left) the day I received the Woolf Institute's 2007 Pursuer of Peace Prize at Middle Temple in London.

Standing shoulder-to-shoulder with Gordon England, America's Deputy Secretary of Defense, in his office at the Pentagon in April 2008.

Below: With my great friend Sheikh Dr Ahmed al-Kubaisi outside his home in Dubai. Samir is with me, as always.

Sheikh Dr Abdel Latif feeling at home in the Cairo Marriott Hotel. The beads he is holding represent the 99 names of God.

Getting down to business in Beirut in 2008 Arab-style, four of Iraq's most senior religious leaders: (clockwise from left) Sheikh Dr al-Kubaisi, Sheikh Dr Abdel Latif, Sheikh al-Zuhairi and Ayatollah Ammar Abu Ragif.

Ayatollah Abu Ragif with Samir, signing the first ever *fatwa* against violence issued jointly by Sunna and Shia.

With Lord Hylton (left), when he presented my foundation's 2008 Prize for Peace in the Middle East to Dr Mowaffak (right) in Baghdad.

The 'most wonderful church in the world' is the congregation, certainly not the building! Since the end of 2004, the latter has been surrounded by concrete blocks, concrete-filled oil drums and razor wire.

Waiting to leave St George's with a few of my people and four of my bodyguards from the Iraqi special forces.

With Majid (on my right), then lay pastor of St George's, and his family at the baptism of his daughter in 2006. He was kidnapped shortly after. On my left stands Colonel Hoyt.

Showing Michael Lewis, our new bishop, around the church on his first ever visit to Baghdad.

With little Vivian in Amman on the joyful day when she came out of hospital after major surgery.

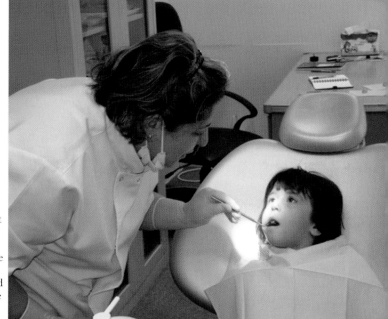

The first patient in the new dental clinic at St George's. The local American commander said its facilities were the best he had seen in Iraq.

Six young people from St George's on a visit to heaven – or, at least, Coventry Cathedral – in 2008: with Samir, me and my son Jacob are (left to right) Osama, David, Sally (holding a replica of the Cross of Nails), Lina, Fulla and Mabel.

With the distinguished British-Somali reporter Rageh Omar outside the door to my home in the Green Zone. He presented a one-hour documentary about me for ITV at the beginning of 2008, titled *The Vicar of Baghdad*.

but also the so-called Mecca Document. This was the product of an independent initiative sponsored by the international Organization of the Islamic Conference, which had been approved by Grand Ayatollah al-Sistani and endorsed by the Grand Imam of al-Azhar, Sheikh Tantawi. It affirmed that 'the blood, property, honour and reputation of Muslims', as well as *all* places of worship, are sacrosanct, prohibited abuse and vilification, called for the release of all hostages and the return of all the displaced, both Muslim and non-Muslim, and quoted the words of God in the Qur'an: 'Reconciliation is best.' Sheikh Abdel Halimjawad Kadhum al-Zuhairi, who chaired the gathering of 29 Sunni and Shia scholars who signed this document live on Iraqi television in 2006 (and who was subsequently appointed chief religious adviser to the Prime Minister Nuri al-Maliki), has worked with us since October 2007.

A weakness of our second Baghdad accord was that as all of Iraq's most senior Sunni leaders now live in exile, none of them had been able to attend and so it did not carry any of their signatures. For that reason, in August 2007 we brought a handful of them together in Cairo, along with one of Grand Ayatollah al-Sistani's most senior men, Ayatollah Ammar Abu Ragif, himself a crucial new participant in this process. It is normal in Arabic culture for the most exalted people to send representatives to meetings, but in this case both Sheikh Dr Ahmed al-Kubaisi and Sheikh Dr Abdel Latif came in person. Few of these men had even met each other before, and a great deal of mutual distrust had to be overcome. Moreover, these were all people who bitterly opposed the American presence in Iraq and had previously refused to meet any representative of the Coalition – and yet here they were engaging with my colleague Colonel Hoyt. (They do accept the US Army chaplains as religious leaders in their own right, though it has not been easy to integrate these Americans into the reconciliation process because they are also soldiers, and look like soldiers. When one of them showed up at a meeting in army boots, some of the Iraqis took me aside and said, 'Those are the boots that kicked down our doors.')

In the end, after long discussion, these very senior men confirmed their support for the two Baghdad accords of 2004 and 2007 and decided to become, in effect, an implementation committee for everything that had been agreed. They then added their own commitment, 'to end terrorist violence and disband militia activity in order to build a civilized country and work within the framework of law', and resolved to seek to involve 'the highest-level religious leaders as soon as possible' and 'engage with other influential and proactive religious leaders with the highest qualifications in order to work towards issuing a comprehensive *fatwa*'. Implicitly, they also urged other senior Sunni leaders to return to Iraq from exile to add their weight to the push for reconciliation (as I believe Sheikh Dr al-Kubaisi and Sheikh Dr Abdel Latif themselves will do one day). It was a simple statement, but one that could have profound consequences.

By this point, the much-heralded 'surge' had at last begun to take effect in Baghdad and the so-called

Sunni Triangle. 'The New Way Forward', as it was more formally known, had actually started at the beginning of the year. The multinational forces in Iraq had been reinforced with about 30,000 American soldiers, most of them deployed in Baghdad. The new strategy had a new focus: to help the Iraqis to take the lead in protecting their own neighbourhoods. The Iraqi army was still predominantly Shia, but a lot of Sunna were now joining it, and with the first-class training its men were receiving from the Coalition it had become a powerful force – far better than the one that had largely melted away before the Coalition in 2003. Dr Mowaffak now made sure that it gave the American troops full support and it began to conduct joint operations with them, including joint patrols led initially by Americans but later on by Iraqis.

General David Petraeus had arrived in Baghdad on 26 January 2007 as commander of the Coalition forces. I would put a lot of the success of the new strategy down to him. He is a wonderful man, quite serious and yet very engaging, and he managed to win the respect of the country's tribal and religious leaders. I had a very good relationship with him. Not least, I found that if I couldn't say something to him in the week I could often say it to him from the pulpit in chapel on Sunday. Whenever my team had an important meeting, I would e-mail him about it and he would always reply – usually, being a soldier, with a one-liner. Another route to him was a subordinate of his called General Moore to whom I used to report everything we did.

At first, the surge had seemed to make no difference to the death toll. On 3 February, a single bomb had slaughtered 135 people in a crowded market in central Baghdad. Over 300 more had been injured. A month later, a string of attacks on Shia pilgrims had left 137 dead and 310 wounded in one day. One effect the surge did have was to displace the violence further afield, even to the Kurdish-dominated north (which previously had been quite peaceful), as al-Qa'ida concentrated its attentions on parts of the country where there were not so many soldiers. On 27 March, for example, the deadliest single attack in Iraq since the end of the war killed 152 people in Tal Afar, close to the Syrian border. (The bloodletting continued the next day, when Shia gunmen, including off-duty policemen, roamed the town's Sunni neighbourhoods, handcuffing any men they found and shooting them in the head. At least 70 men were killed in these reprisals, and 40 more were abducted.) Not that the centre of Iraq was quiet: in April, a hundred people were killed in two separate suicide attacks in the Shia holy city of Karbala and a car bomb in Baghdad killed 140. These, of course, were just the massacres that hit the headlines. In fact, the bloodshed continued every day.

Nonetheless, the American strategy began to show results. A crucial development was that many of Iraq's Sunni insurgents in effect changed sides. General Petraeus was told by his intelligence in al-Anbar that the Sunna there felt that the al-Qa'ida men who had been fighting alongside them were taking control of their province and were now a bigger threat to their communities than either the Coalition or Iraq's Shia-led government. He asked me to enlist the help of Sheikh Dr Abdel Latif, who has a lot of influence with the Sunni sheikhs and tribal leaders, and I spent many hours explaining the general's plans to him. Soon, armed men – whom the Americans called 'concerned local citizens' – were reasserting control of their streets, not only in al-Anbar but also in Baghdad and the adjacent provinces of Babil, Diyala, Salahuddin and Nineva. They became known as 'the Sons of Iraq', or 'Tribal Awakening'. By April 2008, more than 95,000 people were involved, including Shia as well as Sunna. Almost all of them were under contract to the US Army and were being paid $300 a month to maintain law and order.

This strategy has not been uncontroversial, and critics in the West have said that it is buying short-term peace at the cost of encouraging tribalism, 'warlordism' and sectarianism. The Prime Minister, Nuri al-Maliki, has warned that these 'concerned local citizens' are an armed Sunni opposition in the making. A different way of looking at it is that, as one senior Sunni leader put it to me, by giving people authority and respect as well as money General Petraeus has given them back their country. The fact is that this is the only way to get peace in many parts of Iraq – and it has succeeded. The millions of dollars this has cost first the Pentagon and then, since October 2008, the Iraqi government is much less than the cost of the mayhem that would otherwise have continued unabated. Nonetheless, the peace is still fragile and could easily be lost if it was

taken for granted. The Iraqi government has promised
to incorporate 20 per cent of the Sons of Iraq into the
regular armed forces and to go on paying the rest
until they can find civilian jobs, but I would prefer to
see them all taken into the army.

At one point, the Pentagon even asked me if we
could form our own Christian 'sons of Iraq'. I said
that this was not appropriate: perhaps in America
armed Christians might patrol the streets, but not
in the Middle East! Sadly, the plight of the country's
Christians became very much worse in 2006, when
they began to be targeted in earnest by the Muslim
militias. At one point in 2007, an American officer
in the al-Dora neighbourhood of Baghdad said that
over 500 Christians were being murdered there every
month. All the churches there were closed down, and
there was a great exodus. Once, there were reckoned
to be some 700,000 Christians in the country, though
by early 2003 the sanctions and the war had already
driven maybe 200,000 abroad. Today, no more than
55,000 remain. Many have fled, to Jordan, Syria or
Lebanon or to the West – especially Sweden, where for
a while it was very easy to get asylum. Increasingly, it
is only the poorest who are still left in Iraq. The same
is true for the country's other religious minorities.
Most of the 25,000 Mandeans counted in the 1997
national census have now gone, for example – and of
the 109 Jews who lived in Iraq in 1997, the last of a
community that dates back to the time of the Second
Exile in Babylon in the sixth century BC, just eight
remain in the country today. As the tiniest of Iraq's

minorities, they are very fearful for the future.

Between the Shia and the Sunna, however, the conflict has begun to abate. In the period from June to November 2007, the monthly death toll nationwide fell by 70 per cent. As well as the surge, I believe that our work for reconciliation was beginning to bear fruit. Consider the reaction to the successive attacks on the al-Askari Mosque in Samarra, which is venerated by the Sunna but is especially sacred to the Shia as it contains the tombs of the tenth and eleventh Imams. In February 2006, when its golden dome was destroyed by bombs, a string of reprisals across the country claimed thousands of Sunni lives. In June 2007 – actually during the press conference that followed our first II-RC summit in Baghdad – the mosque was attacked again and two of its minarets were blown up. All of our delegates, Sunna as well as Shia, joined in condemning this. A month later, the mosque's clock tower was also blown up. Remarkably, no one was killed in retaliation. Muqtada al-Sadr responded to the provocation by saying he did not believe that Sunni Arabs could be responsible and called for three days of mourning and peaceful demonstrations. In August, after our Cairo meeting issued its denunciation of al-Qa'ida, the ranks of the Sons of Iraq were noticeably swelled, while on the Shia side Muqtada al-Sadr ordered his Mehdi Army to cease fighting.

Seven months later, he sent his chief spokesman, Sheikh Salah al-Ubaidi, to our next round of discussions in Cairo. In spite of everything, we seemed to be making progress!

CHAPTER 5

....

Knowing the Right People

E VEN SO, THERE WERE STILL NEW depths of horror to plumb. On 14 August 2007, suicide bombers, almost certainly from al-Qa'ida, detonated a fuel tanker and three other vehicles packed with explosives in the Yazidi villages of al-Qataniya and al-Adnaniya, in the north-west of the country near Mosul. Many of the houses, which were built of clay and stone, were completely flattened, burying those inside. Someone at the scene said that it looked like the aftermath of a nuclear explosion. Initial estimates of 250 dead soon rose to more than 500, with as many as 1,500 more injured. The Americans eventually put the death toll at 796.

The victims belonged to the ancient community, mainly Kurdish but defined by their religion, that lives in villages around Lalish and spread out across northern Iraq. It is reckoned that there are just over 200,000 Yazidi in the country, which is maybe half of their total number worldwide. They are often regarded as Devil worshippers, but this is based on a misunderstanding. They revere a being they call Melek Taus, the Peacock Angel, whom they also know as Shaytan – which is the name the Qur'an gives to the Devil. Yazidi generally get on well with Iraq's Christians, but the more extreme Muslims hate them and have often attacked both them and Christians together. Unfortunately, most Yazidi are very poor and could not afford to leave Iraq even if they wanted to. The threat to them increased considerably in April 2007 after a 17-year-old Yazidi woman was stoned to death by her community, reportedly for wanting to convert to Islam so that she could marry a young Muslim. Shortly after, 23 mostly elderly Yazidi men were taken off a bus in Mosul, lined up against a wall and shot to death.

So it continued. In October, a suicide bomber on a bicycle massacred 30 police recruits in Baquba, in the eastern province of Diyala, which had seen a big increase in violence since the surge began. (On the same day, close by the same city, 20 headless corpses were discovered but could not be identified.) In December, two suicide bombers targeted Awakening patrols in Diyala and Salahuddin, killing 33 people and wounding another 77. There was a growing number of suicide attacks on the queues of young men throughout the country who – desperate for work and desperate for peace – were trying to join the security forces. The new year saw a horrible new development: on 2 February 2008, two bombs strapped to women with Down's syndrome were set off by remote control, killing 99 people in two pet markets in Baghdad. These were the city's worst attacks in six months and seemed to mark a new level of depravity. Three weeks later, in the ancient city of Iskandariya, a suicide bomber killed 63 pilgrims on their way to one of the holiest of Shia festivals.

It was in February 2008 that we held another major conference in Copenhagen, at the invitation of its Lutheran bishop. The Danish government paid for this. There are several reasons why our work has won support from this country. First, I live next door to its embassy in Baghdad; its ambassador until recently, Bo Eric Weber, is a very good friend of mine, and his deputy, Torqild Byg, is the longest-standing member of my Anglican congregation in the chapel at the Palace. A second factor is that after a Welsh woman living in Denmark contacted me about the plight of Iraqi asylum seekers there, her church began to support my foundation and eventually the Danish government allowed her pastor, Niels Eriksen, to come and visit me in Baghdad. There is now a memorial fountain in the garden of St George's that lists the names of all the Danish soldiers who have been killed in Iraq.

The Iraqi Reconciliation Conference brought together the broadest range of delegates yet, including Christians, Yazidi and Mandeans as well as Sunna and Shia, and Armenians and Assyrians as well as Arabs and Kurds. There were also politicians from the Council of Ministers and the Council of Representatives, including Dr Mowaffak and Mrs Wijdan. As well as issues of human rights (in particular, for women and children), there was frank discussion of the proper role of religion in government. Several people – members of the government and religious leaders – who had previously refused to be reconciled were so.

This gathering took place within a few days of the reprinting by many Danish newspapers of the notorious cartoon of the Prophet Muhammad with a bomb in his turban, after the police apparently foiled a plot to murder the man who drew it. Many of the Muslim delegates threatened to boycott the conference as a result, but in the end we persuaded all but three to come. The Danish government, to its credit, was all the more determined that the event should go ahead. The three days bore fruit in a strong statement signed by everyone who attended which presented their detailed vision for the future of Iraq and how this might be realized.

The following month, on 13–16 March, the third of the Pentagon-sponsored II-RC meetings took place, again in Cairo. This time, 18 people were present, including Sheikh al-Zuhairi, Muqtada al-Sadr's lieutenant Sheikh al-Ubaidi and representatives of the reclusive Grand Ayatollah al-Sistani as well as some very senior Sunni clerics. The statement they issued announced a total rejection of all violence. It was a major achievement. As well as the formal outcomes of such meetings, however, the informal business that goes on between sessions is just as important. On the last evening, we were all crammed into a small bus on our way to a final meal together when one of the Sunni sheikhs started singing a Sunni religious song and one by one the others joined in. When Ayatollah Abu Ragif asked them to sing a Shia song, there was a moment of tension before they obliged and then everyone, Sunni and Shia, began laughing and singing. It was amazing how different the atmosphere was after the mutual suspicion of the first day. When the same sheikh launched into a song about Fatima, the wife of Imam Ali, who is especially revered by the Shia, Ayatollah Abu Ragif began to cry. He told us afterwards that he loves Fatima so much and it touched him to hear Sunna and Shia singing about her together.

Later that evening, Peter Maki was chatting to a delegate who was representing al-Fadhila, the Shia party led by Ayatollah Muhammad Ya'qubi whose militia has sometimes clashed with the Mehdi Army. This man confessed that he had heard many things about Sheikh Dr Abdel Latif and his links with Saddam and had been prepared to hate him; yet, having talked to him and eaten with him, he now appreciated that the sheikh was a delightful man who, like him, wanted to end his country's torment. He was going to tell Ayatollah Ya'qubi, he said, that they could put the past behind them and work together to build a free Iraq. The same man also mentioned that a close relative of his had been jailed over a month before by the Americans, who had given no explanation except that they needed to question him. It hurt his heart, he told Peter, to see things like this happen that undermined all the good that democracy had brought to Iraq – and yet, he said, he was still willing to engage with the Coalition.

Within days, however – as if to demonstrate the ambiguities of peacemaking in Iraq – there was heavy fighting on the streets of Basra as the Iraqi army made a concerted effort to wrest control of the country's only port from the Mehdi Army and restore law and order. This, too, was highly significant – a massive onslaught on A Shia militia ordered by a Shia-led administration. Finally, after six days, the Mehdi Army requested a ceasefire and withdrew its gunmen from the streets, and things began to quieten down.

Since then, things have progressed quickly. I have been in contact with the key Sunni and Shia leaders almost every day, and we meet with them every two months; but the greatest advance is that every other month they meet each other without us. Meanwhile, other good work has continued at the grass roots, where our allies at the US Institute of Peace and others have had remarkable success. Of the working parties established by the Baghdad Conference in June 2007, all but one are still meeting regularly. Sadly, after we had done a huge amount of preparatory research, we had to disband the one devoted to reconstruction as everyone vainly expected the Coalition to pay for all the work. The most active of the working parties is one that the Iraqi religious leaders themselves insisted upon, which deals with the welfare of women and children.

Finally, in August 2008, I met with the most senior II-RC delegates in Beirut. Of the five we had expected, only Muqtada al-Sadr's representative did not turn up. Although they expressed their distress and frustration that 'nothing had happened' in 2006 and 2007, there was now a sense that the time had come to work seriously and resolutely for peace. The great prize of those five days together was the first ever *fatwa* against violence issued jointly by Sunna and Shia:

In Islam it is known that our God of mercy has chosen and blessed Adam's sons more than all other created beings (Holy Qur'an, al-Isra 70).

It is known that all Muslims are totally prohibited from harming anybody, as stated in the Holy Qur'an, al-Ma'ida 32.

The Prophet Muhammad prohibited the spilling of blood by a Muslim against a Muslim. Therefore, all suicide bombings are totally prohibited.

Therefore, as Sunni and Shia religious leaders, we declare that all killing must be stopped now. We also declare that the killing of non-Muslims is also totally unacceptable. The process of reconciliation and tolerance is the only way forward and the only solution to the conflict in Iraq. This is also seen in the Holy Qur'an, in al-Hujurat 9. We see it as both our religious and our ethical duty to urge people to hold to shari'a *law and to see it as a refuge and the only solution to the conflict. We acknowledge that these are difficult times but we demand that all violence, killing and provocation be stopped. We ask that all involved in violence join with us to support reconciliation and tolerance, in accordance with al-Nisa 65 in the Holy Qur'an.*

It is the ethical and religious duty of all Iraqis to abandon all violence and live under the rule of law. This is our fatwa *to all Iraqi people and all Muslims. From our God we have been told, and have delivered this message, may our God be our witness!*

After the war, I had been concerned to forge relationships with as many of Iraq's religious leaders as I could. However, although it is essential in Arabic culture to maintain good relations, once formed, in order to prevent friends from actually becoming enemies, our emphasis today is on *reducing* the number we are dealing with, so that we can concentrate on the absolutely key people. Unlike the Sunna, the Shia have a religious hierarchy, not dissimilar to the Roman Catholics. There are five *Maraje* (who are the supreme legal authorities in Shia Islam) living in Iraq today. The most senior of these is Grand Ayatollah Ali al-Sistani, who has enjoyed that pre-eminence since 1999, when his predecessor, Muqtada al-Sadr's father, was assassinated by Saddam's agents. He lives in the holy city of Najaf, along with the ayatollahs closest to him, and he declines to meet anyone who is not an Iraqi. However, I am told by Dr Mowaffak and Ayatollah al-Sadr that he strongly approves of our work – and since 2007 one of his key people, Ayatollah Abu Ragif, has been attending our meetings.

Grand Ayatollah Muhammad Taqi al-Modarresi is the leading authority in Karbala, the second Iraqi city that the Shia consider holy. I have met with him, as I have with Grand Ayatollah Muhammad Sayed al-Hakim, who commands the powerful militia of the Supreme Council for the Islamic Revolution in Iraq, better known as Sciri. I have never met Iraq's other two grand ayatollahs, Bashir Hussein al-Najafi and Muhammad Ishaq al-Fayyad, but Ayatollah Abu Ragif is close to them.

In Baghdad, by far the most important Shia is Ayatollah Hussein al-Sadr, who presides over the third-holiest Shia shrine in Iraq, the al-Khadamiya Mosque, and exerts influence through his own TV channel. He has been committed to peace from the beginning, and remains my closest spiritual ally in Iraq. His nephew Muqtada al-Sadr is not a senior cleric, but is important because he controls the Mehdi Army, the largest militia in Iraq. He doesn't attend our meetings (though he has rung me more than once), but he sends his chief spokesman in his place.

Among the Sunna, there are three sheikhs who are supremely important: Dr Ahmed al-Kubaisi, Dr Abdel Latif Humayem and Dr Harith al-Dari. Of these, only the last, who is the head of the Association of Muslim Scholars, has not honoured his commitment to work with us for peace. He now lives in Syria and Jordan, and we no longer have anything to do with him.

Sheikh Dr al-Kubaisi has been to Iraq only once since the war. He lives in great luxury in several houses in Dubai, where he fled after falling out with Saddam many years ago. At the age of over 70, he has just become the father of twins! He exerts huge influence in Iraq through his almost daily television

programmes. I have a really warm relationship with
him, and believe that he is committed to what we are
trying to achieve. His principal lieutenant in Iraq was
Sheikh Dr Abdel Qadir al-Ani, who worked with us in
the early days after the war but then fled to Jordan in
2004 after his house was bombed and he was accused
of being a traitor and collaborator. He comes to most
of our meetings in Amman.

Sheikh Dr Abdel Latif, too, has been back to Iraq
only once since the fall of Saddam, in 2004 (when he
was greeted with remarkable warmth by Ayatollah al-
Sadr). The reason he gives is that the National De-
Ba'thification Committee (chaired by Ahmed Chalabi,
who is not exactly beyond reproach himself) then
seized all his assets, amounting to over $70 million,
and he can no longer afford security for himself. Today
he lives in Amman, in a fairly modest apartment, while
I work hard with the Americans to restore his fortune
to him. He has played a crucial role in reducing Sunni
violence. His genuine commitment to the cause of
peace and reconciliation, which is rooted in his ten-
year relationship with me, has strengthened since
we introduced him to Ayatollah Abu Ragif in Cairo.
They have become not only allies but friends, which
is a perfect example of what the FRRME has been
trying to achieve. He will never enjoy the amount of
influence and prestige he had as Saddam's personal
imam, because Iraq is a democracy now and the
Sunna are a minority; but we have been able to give
him something back of what he lost in 2003.

The Foundation for Relief and Reconciliation in the Middle East, which I launched with the former Archbishop of Canterbury George Carey in June 2005, just before I quit my job at Coventry Cathedral, is now the vehicle for everything I do. Lord Carey, its original chair, continues to work very closely with us as its patron. Our trustees are now chaired by David Harland, the pastor of a church in Brighton that strongly supports us, and we also have an outstanding board of advisers who meet with me regularly in central London. This group is made up of Christians, Jews and Muslims and has a mix of businesspeople, religious leaders, peacemakers and diplomats, including several former British ambassadors to the Middle East. Its chair is Lord Hylton, a Roman Catholic peer who has a strong interest in that part of the world. It is with this group that I discuss the practicalities of our work, and their advice is invaluable.

In America we have a similar board of advisers who likewise meet regularly, chaired by Robert 'Bud' McFarlane, who was Ronald Reagan's National Security Advisor from 1983 to 1985. Many of its members are people we have worked with in Iraq, and Bud himself has attended many of our gatherings of Iraq's religious leaders, including the key ones in Cairo and Beirut. Whether we have met in Iraq itself or in Lebanon, Egypt or Jordan, he has been there to give us insight and direction. He is a man of wisdom, who survived the disgrace that followed the Iran-Contra scandal to become a very committed Christian.

Bud is a friend of John McCain, having served with him in Vietnam, and as a result I often receive messages of support and encouragement from the senator, who even promised me that if he became President he would meet all of the key Iraqi leaders I am working with. (When I mentioned this to them, they each started telling me in private that they were the most important and should meet the President on their own!) There is no question that the outcome of the American election will have more impact on the streets of Baghdad than it will on those of Washington or New York. I have been deeply impressed by Barack Obama as a person, but I was most struck by Senator McCain's words, 'I'm a great believer in reconciliation and redemption.' I can't deny that for the sake of Iraq I hoped and prayed that he would win.

In 2008, the FRRME awarded its Prize for Peace in the Middle East to Dr Mowaffak, in recognition of the crucial part he had played in our work for the past five years, not only as chair of the IIP but also as my principal adviser and one of my closest friends. The presentation was made twice: in Baghdad by Lord Hylton and in London at the House of Lords by Lord Carey.

We have spent so much time and effort working for the healing of a whole nation, and yet so often our highest priority from one day to the next has been to try to save a few individual lives. To date, I and my team have been involved in negotiations for a total of 142 victims of kidnapping. Ninety-eight of these were taken for money, and we managed to get 30 of them released. The other 44 were abducted for political reasons, and sadly we have so far got only nine of them back.

In the second category are five men who have preoccupied me since 29 May 2007, all of them Britons. Four of my bodyguards from GardaWorld were protecting an IT consultant at the Ministry of Finance in Baghdad when they were all kidnapped by dozens of men, some in uniform, who arrived in a large fleet of police cars. Ever since that day, it has been the highest priority in my work to try to locate them and secure their release. My trailer is inside the GardaWorld compound, and these men lived opposite me. Not only were they my protectors, they are my friends. One of them, who had been a medic in the Army, was meant to have started at medical school in south London in September 2007. As this book goes to press, in February 2009, they have still not been found or freed. I have had meeting after meeting, with so many different people. Literally every day I work on their case, and it has seriously affected our other work, not least in Israel/Palestine. I can never make an absolute commitment to be anywhere or do anything, because I have to drop everything if something comes up in connection with these hostages. Everything else has to be provisional.

In a spiritual update in May 2008, I wrote this:

The past year has been very difficult and until now
I have not been able to talk about it. At times I have
not even been able to communicate with people.
This has been because of the search for the five

British hostages. The 29th of May will mark the first anniversary [of their kidnap]. All year we have been working on this case non-stop. It has been very difficult – it took us six months even to get on the right lines. You can never say for certain that you are dealing with the right people, but it now looks as if we are.

In the last year, I have spent a huge amount of my own money and the Foundation's money on [this matter]. To date, we have spent nearly $700,000 ... to meet with the right people, and even to bring people in from Iran. Paying for security [for them] has been immensely expensive. We have not been able to ask for people to support these initiatives – it has all been carried out in secret with just a few people praying for us. On Sunday I had a secret meeting at the church with people from Iran. It cost $50,000 just to have this meeting. It was difficult, but [at least now] we had clear demands, one of which was to go public [and talk to the media]. Despite there being no ransom demand, both the [Foreign Office and GardaWorld] had wanted to keep everything quiet. ...

Yesterday was one of the most difficult days of my life. It all looked so awful, as if the whole venture would be lost. I felt very angry and wanted to tell [GardaWorld] I wanted to give up and their attitude was totally wrong. I sat down to send the e-mail and God told me not to send it. I had an e-mail from a friend in the USA telling me to love, love and love. I agreed with this as regards the really bad guys, but did this apply to governments and companies as well? God said yes, it did. I did not send the e-mail and knew that it was now up to God.

Such a hard day followed. I struggled, I prayed continually. I was not focused. In the afternoon, I met with people from the US chapel and St George's, including many of the children. This really lifted my spirits. Samir told me we could not give up. I agreed, not because I felt like continuing but because I knew that was what our Lord was saying. I returned to base yesterday evening to hear that everything had changed. Both the British Government and the company had agreed that we should go ahead with our plan. So, for the first time, I will soon – not yet – be able to talk about this case. For the first time since the kidnapping I will be able to talk to the media.

We are told that following an active [media] campaign there will be a release. The kidnappers have said that 11 times they have been approached by the Iraqi government but have refused to engage with them. They said they decided to deal with me because they knew of my involvement in the Bethlehem siege resolution and because I was a religious leader. Since then, most of our meetings have happened in secret at the church. The security has been immense, but secret. Soldiers have literally hidden and watched from rooftops and inside the church. Our church people have always prayed fervently in these meetings. Our staff have cared for and looked after our visitors, feeding them well.

We now need your prayer fervently in the next month. I will return to the UK next week to start working on this campaign. In a short while, I will be able to talk to the media about this issue. First, though, we need to make a video that will be widely distributed. So, we enter another really important period. I ask your prayer for Al, Alan, Jason, Jason and Peter, the five [hostages]. Please pray that we will get them back soon. We are told that if the kidnappers are happy with what we do they will soon be returned.

In many ways, this case is typical of much of what we are doing here. Nothing is quickly achieved and nothing is certain. We will not even know for sure that we are dealing with the right people until these hostages are actually returned to us. The search for them has already cost us so much in both time and money. But I will not give up. Every Thursday the people of St George's meet to pray for their release, and it will happen. I cannot go into the details of what we are doing to secure it, but one day I will be able to tell the whole tale.

Their story is a tiny sample of the ordeal that Iraq has suffered since 2003. Today, it seems that more and more people in the West condemn the invasion of Iraq. The cost in human lives has greatly exceeded what almost anyone predicted, and the cost in billions of dollars vastly so. So many people say to me: 'Look at the situation now! How can you say the war was not a terrible mistake?' I can say it easily, because I saw this country before the war. I witnessed the oppression, felt the intense, pervasive sense of fear. I heard people whispering that they needed to be released from tyranny. I will never forget the horror in my Mukhabarat minder's face when I told him I would not have dinner with Saddam's sons. If I didn't go, he said, he and his family would all be killed. It was then I understood just how evil that regime was.

I am not saying that everything in Iraq is rosy now, because it is not. So many times I have sat on my bed at night and cried over the death of an American or Iraqi friend. At times, I have thought that the suffering was just too much to bear. Then I remember that we are engaged in the rebuilding of a nation. Yes, there is still fear, but there is also hope. We know that one day this will again be the great country that it used to be. Unless you have been here, you cannot imagine the pain Iraq has gone through – but unless you have been here you also cannot have any idea how much good has already been achieved. Despite all the violence, the work of building or restoring hospitals, power stations, schools and roads has gone on. Most civilian contractors have long ago fled Iraq, despite the huge sums of money they were paid; today, the construction work is being done by the US Army – often by reservists, men and women with other jobs and other lives who are making great sacrifices to serve both their country and the Iraqi people.

As I write this in October 2008, it has been announced that last month 359 civilians were killed in

Iraq, compared with 884 in September 2007. This is a measure of how much the situation here has improved – and of how terrible it still is. This is still the most dangerous country in the world. Baghdad is still the most dangerous city in the world. Even now, some of the children from St George's have just rung me to say that this morning two large bombs went off near their school and they were showered with glass as all the windows in the building shattered. Some people are dead. It is another normal day. Nonetheless, the violence *is* diminishing. I know this not just because the statistics say so but because my congregation tells me so. In the Green Zone, where I live, we used to be bombarded with rockets every day; now, such attacks are rare. Things have changed enormously for the better, though this has yet to be recognized by the international media. It is still not possible for ordinary people to walk down the streets of Baghdad or Mosul in safety, there are still murders and abductions every day, and yet the fact is that order is slowly but surely being restored – and we hope and pray that peace and reconciliation will follow.

CHAPTER 6

....

Giving Peace
a Chance

ALMOST EVERY DAY I AM contacted by people
who want to talk to me about peacemaking.
Often they have good ideas – they want to
develop inter-community relations, perhaps to host
some sports activity that would bring together young
people of different religions, races or tribes. Initiatives
like these are important, but I have to confess I have
very little experience in this area. In Iraq, to be honest,
I have learned that the established strategies for
resolving conflict – working through political issues,
restoring civil society, supporting the moderates,
involving women – are mostly ineffectual. What is more
productive, I have found, is to gain an understanding
specifically of the people who are responsible for the
violence and of their culture, religion, traditions and
everything that shapes their expectations. These are
the influences that propel people into conflict; these
are the factors that complicate its resolution.

In the early days after the liberation of Iraq, so much of what we did was aimed at finding political solutions that we thought would engineer change and generate hope. It would have been wonderful if those initiatives had worked, but most of them did not. Of the six working parties set up by the Iraqi Centre for Dialogue, Reconciliation and Peace in early 2004, for example, only the one concerned with women, religion and democracy ever bore much fruit. Some of the key women's leaders we identified were subsequently elected to Iraq's new parliament and did a very important job – though now they tell us that their male colleagues only laugh at them. Mrs Samia Aziz Mohamed, the Faili Kurd who led this effort for us and became an MP herself, lost three of her relatives and her house in 2006 in an attack by Shia gunmen.

So much of my work now is about helping people simply to stay alive, and to keep their remaining loved ones alive, amidst the constant violence. There is no knowing how many people have been killed, or even how many have been abducted, since the fall of Baghdad in 2003. Those who are taken are very rarely returned. The humanitarian situation, too, is dire. People often ask me why my foundation is involved in relief work. The answer is simple: because no one else is. Those foreign aid workers who were here in the heart of Iraq have fled. Many have gone to the north of the country, to the beauty and comparative peace of Kurdistan. They tell their supporters they are working in Iraq and of course it is true – but they are in a different world from the one we are operating in.

Many of these people work for Christian agencies. They were not wrong to leave central Iraq – they had to. It would have been far too dangerous for them to remain here. If they had stayed, they would have achieved little and most probably would have been seen as missionaries trying to convert Muslims. They themselves would then have been at serious risk of being kidnapped or murdered, while any Iraqi Christians associated with them would have been reckoned as supporters of the 'Crusader' ideology of the West. This is the perspective of militant Muslims who do not realize that Christianity took root here long before Islam, and long before it took root in the West. Such thinking is dangerously prevalent here.

The flight of the major relief organizations from the heart of this country has increased the burden on the FRRME massively. Fighting for peace in the Middle East is always hard, but at times in Iraq it is soul-destroying. So, what is the role of a peacemaker in this country, amidst the trauma and chaos that have become so normal here? You soon discard the idea that success may come quickly: any strategy has to be long-term. You are also soon disabused of the idea that imposing Western-style democracy will bring peace. Whenever a democratic system has been introduced to the Middle East in the recent past, the outcome has generally been bad. Democracy has given Iran a malignant president and Gaza a terrorist government, and Iraq, too, has suffered enormously because it took so long for people to agree on who should run it. In fact, the most stable governments in the region are those of Morocco and Jordan, which are essentially benevolent hereditary dictatorships.

Attempts by the West to foster peace in the Middle East by encouraging democracy show that our politicians have not considered the core values of these societies, and in particular their religious identity, their culture of honour and shame, the influence of the family and the pervasive role of tradition. Many of our Western ideals simply do not work in this part of the world. It sounds very fine, for example, to try to bring about change from the bottom up, and in the West it may work; but here it does not. Here, the only way you can really effect change is to work from the top down. In particular, it is the religious leaders who determine which way a society will go – and in order to influence them we have to make friends with them. This, I believe, has been our most crucial mistake in the West: we have failed to understand that at the heart of Middle Eastern society is the idea of relationship, which means that establishing and nurturing relationships have to be absolutely central to our work.

What is important is not only how strong our relationships are but who they are with. We can make progress in peacemaking only when we are engaging with the key people on both – or all – sides of the conflict. In Israel/Palestine, that is comparatively easy; but in Iraq it is much more complex. The parties to the violence include the Sunna, the Shia, the Kurds, the Americans and their partners in the Coalition, and the Iraqi government and its security forces. Moreover, there is fighting not only between communities but also within them, as different factions struggle for control. Everyone needs to be involved in the quest for peace. Peacemaking of the old woolly-liberal kind no longer works, if it ever did. We cannot succeed if we do not engage with the military. By the same token, we have to engage too with the people who choose to kidnap women and children and blow up buses. We cannot confine ourselves to sitting down and drinking tea with nice people.

Not everyone is approachable, of course – some groups, such as al-Qa'ida, are impossible to engage with at any level. How great it would be to meet with them and talk sense, to restore to them what they feel they have lost and seek peace and reconciliation! But that is simply not possible, because it is of no interest to them. They are set only on killing and maiming in the name of God. I have, however, got very close to the most senior people in the Mehdi Army and other such radical groups, and I continue to be so. (This can be quite disconcerting. One day, I was sitting in my study in leafy Hampshire when I had a phone call from Muqtada al-Sadr. He had heard it reported that the Archbishop of Canterbury, Dr Rowan Williams, had said that *shari'a* law should be introduced to England and he wanted me to tell Lambeth Palace how much he approved.) If anyone who is responsible for violence is willing to deal with us, we have to engage with them if we are to have any hope of bringing peace to Iraq. It is often difficult to get these people to meet representatives of the Coalition, because Western governments do not want to be seen to be talking to 'the bad guys' – though in private they are glad we are doing it, and the Pentagon especially is now happy to finance this aspect of our work.

I am involved with both religious and political leaders and I find they often fail to understand each other. Western politicians do not appreciate that religious extremists need to be addressed in religious language. On the other hand, most religious leaders have little insight into the nature of Western politics and are unaware that most of our politicians find violence in the name of God incomprehensible. Often, a further obstacle to mutual understanding is the belief shared by both kinds of leader that the only way to deal with the other kind is by force. Both of them tend to assume that if you hurt someone enough they will submit to your will. The problem with this assumption is that usually it results only in an escalation of violence.

There is no simple formula, no secret, to getting these people to engage with us or with each other, or to change their tactics; and there is little rhyme or reason in how we have achieved it. It can take months merely to get to know some people – and yet often it is when we get to know them, and even make friends with them, that solutions begin to emerge. Fortunately, Christianity encourages us in this approach, because Jesus taught us to love our enemies and forgive them. (Most of those I deal with in the Middle East, however, are Jews or Muslims, and this concept of loving and forgiving your enemies is foreign to their religion. It can be difficult to explain it to them.)

As a third party, I and my colleagues play a vital

role not only by mediating negotiations but also by facilitating the forming of relationships across the divides. Often, our starting-point is enabling each side to hear the other's story. As the American poet Longfellow once wrote: 'If we could read the secret history of our enemies, we should find in each man's life sorrow and suffering enough to disarm all hostility.' Or, as someone has said, 'Who is my enemy? It is the person whose story I have not heard.' Merely to get to this point of listening to each other can take many months or even years, but once we have reached it we find that people are often astonished to learn of the pain the other side is experiencing in the conflict.

Such encounters may be the beginning of a road that leads to reconciliation, but we need to find a way to keep people moving along it. This may involve arranging regular conferences, seminars or private meetings between religious and political leaders, or it may mean something more informal, such as a meal together. All of this sounds easier than it actually is. In fact, progress can be excruciatingly slow. Once I thought we could achieve things quickly, but it did not take long to discover that in Iraq you have to operate by Middle Eastern, not Western, time. Something that in Britain or America you might hope to accomplish in a day can take over a year here.

In the meantime, our task is often just to get to know people's concerns and to hear them tell their stories in the way they want to tell them. This in itself can be very difficult: time and time again I encounter views I know to be seriously flawed or grossly inaccurate. Everything requires tact and patience. The fact is, however, that while summits can produce stirring declarations (and I have been involved in many of them), on their own they will achieve nothing. It is the individuals that come to such gatherings who can make the difference – as long as we invest enough time and money in working with them. And they, too, need to spend time meeting with others, on their own side and the other side, who also have the influence to make a difference. In August 2007, I met in Cairo with a number of Iraq's most distinguished religious leaders. When Abu Ragif, a Shia ayatollah, and Dr Abdel Latif, a Sunni sheikh, said they wanted to meet at least once a month, I thought they were being far too ambitious – they didn't even live in the same country. And yet that is what has happened. One of Iraq's most senior Shia leaders has been sitting down regularly with one of its most senior Sunni leaders. This is how change is brought about. Declarations are all very well, I have learned, but they must be followed by action – and it is relationships that make this possible.

Once we have established relationships – and set up the congresses or institutes or whatever that will sustain them – we then have to dedicate ourselves to developing them. Every day, we have to address the various issues they throw up, and this involves meeting with all the different parties involved – diplomats, politicians, soldiers, religious leaders and terrorists. Every meeting is different in character.

All of the diplomats I talk to in Iraq work for one or another member of the Coalition. Generally, my engagement on this front is at a very high level, as I usually deal with the ambassador of a country or his deputy. My conversations with these people are always wide-ranging. Some governments are involved in funding specific aspects of our work with religious leaders and so their embassies need to know how these projects are developing, to be assured that their aims are being achieved. Often, I am asked to arrange meetings for them with various sectarian leaders, and sometimes I am able to and sometimes not.

Often my discussions with diplomats focus on ways to reduce political sectarianism and encourage the building of coalitions across the tribal and religious divides. (In Iraq's first democratic election, for a transitional assembly in January 2005, over 120 different groups and parties put up candidates, which was impractical as well as daunting for the voters.) I always leave these meetings with a long list of things to do. My unique ability to relate to Iraq's religious leaders means that when I meet with diplomats from Coalition countries I can inform them of the views I have encountered 'on the ground'. One question that has been central to our deliberations is: How can religion advise, rather than supervise, politics? Often I find that diplomats have only a very limited understanding of the nature of religion in Iraq, and so these meetings can be very educational.

With some diplomats, I am frequently involved in complex hostage negotiations. In these cases, the character of our meetings is totally different. They ask me for details about our dealings with the people we think may be the kidnappers, and sometimes I can give them that information and sometimes I can't. I cannot betray people's trust, even when they are generally perceived as 'really bad' people. It is crucial in such negotiations that everyone recognizes that I and my team are not working for any government. (It is no secret that a large part of my foundation's funding comes from the Pentagon, but the Americans have never once told us what to do and I always make this clear to the people we are dealing with – and they accept this.) We have to approach these matters as religious, not secular, leaders. It is this that wins us respect in Iraq and enables us – not always, but sometimes – to accomplish what we are trying to do.

My relations with Iraqi politicians are not always easy, but they are always very civil. Some of them, such as the National Security Adviser, Dr Mowaffak, I have become very close to. All of Iraq's prime ministers since the war have also become my friends. When I meet with these people, we talk through every aspect of their work and ours, from trying to combat religious sectarianism to caring for my congregation at St George's. I also have to engage with politicians from the various countries in the Coalition, and especially our major partners, America, Britain and Denmark.

My dealings with members of the armed forces, both foreign and (to a much smaller extent) Iraqi, are always precise and to the point, focusing strictly on what needs to be accomplished and how it can be done. The key issue is how the violence can be reduced, for the fact is that the principal peacemakers in Iraq today are the military. Indeed, I often remind them of this fact. Once again, I deal chiefly with the senior officers and have little to do with the lower ranks unless I see them at chapel. I have especially close relations with the American military, both on the ground in Iraq and at the Department of Defense in Washington.

My encounters with religious leaders are always intense. It's essential that I maintain a good relationship with them in whatever country or situation we find ourselves. All of the leaders I work with carry great authority in both the political and the religious sphere, and it is often difficult to get across to them the fact that in the West religious leaders do not have the same influence. Many of these men now live outside Iraq, and so I and my colleagues are constantly flying to other parts of the Middle East. Our endless phone calls are not enough: we have to visit them as often and as regularly as we can – and take them presents, as their culture requires. We spend hours in deep discussions with them about matters relating to Iraq, and usually they have complaints about the multinational forces, the government and other religious groups and leaders. Engaging with these people can be very expensive as well as time-consuming, but it is essential because even those who live in exile still wield great influence through their broadcasts on television and through the major organizations they are involved in running in Iraq.

The most important people I deal with, however, are the terrorists. If our concern is to stem the violence, we have to work with those who perpetrate it. As I have said already, this is not always easy, or even possible, and there are groups such as al-Qa'ida that refuse to engage with the Coalition except in battle. In these cases, armed force is the only remaining option. Many people object to the idea that military action has an important role in peacemaking, but I believe it is true more strongly now than ever. In other cases, however, you realize that there are non-aggressive ways to pacify people. For example, many Iraqis have resorted to violence because they perceive that something precious has been taken from them. They may have lost territory, money, prestige or political influence, but in the end it all boils down to a loss of power. The solution is some sort of concession. To win them over to the cause of peace, we have to persuade the Coalition and the Iraqi government to give them something back. I can't reveal what this has meant in practice – regrettably, for security reasons, much of what we do cannot be disclosed. All I can say is that mediating the negotiations that this entails constitutes a major part of my work and it is often very complex and time-consuming.

It is essential in all this that people come to trust me and my colleagues. This does not happen automatically. A crucial factor is that first and foremost I am regarded as a religious leader. That is the only reason I can do this job. If I were not a priest, I could not do it. I am frequently told by members of the Iraqi government that my two most important qualifications for my work are that I am myself a cleric and that I have been in Iraq for a long time, now over a decade.

It makes all the difference that I am ordained because here there is very little distinction between religion and politics. In the West we may talk about the separation of church and state and it may have big advantages, but the reality in Iraq – as, indeed, in much of the non-Western world – is very different. Recently, when one of my team asked some of Grand Ayatollah al-Sistani's people what they thought of Iraq's new government, they told him matter-of-factly, '*We* are the government.' Here in Iraq, religion and politics are inextricably entwined. I was in a discussion group with Madeleine Albright at the launch of the Clinton Global Initiative in 2005 and she admitted that her biggest mistake in office, as America's Secretary of State from 1997 to 2001, was not to take seriously the role of religion in diplomatic affairs. As she points out in her brilliant book *The Mighty and the Almighty*, it is futile to try to 'keep religion out of politics'. It is bound up in so much of the conflict in our world and we cannot be serious about peacemaking unless we are serious about engaging with it.

The mutual incomprehension between the Islamic world and the West is certainly one of the biggest problems facing humankind today. Many Muslims do not understand the fundamentals of Western society. They see it in simple terms, as recklessly secular, with no God-given ideals. Unfortunately, this perception is confirmed by much of our television, whose witness they see and believe. You only have to watch a little Arabic TV to see the difference. (Curiously, the divorce between religion and politics in the West goes even deeper in those countries where it is unofficial, such as Britain, than it does in America, where it is established by the constitution.)

The West, in return, has many false perceptions of Islam, which it associates increasingly with radicalism and terrorism. We forget that for hundreds of years Christians, too, waged war in the name of God. Violence in God's name is always wrong, whoever it is committed by, but we need to grasp that only a small percentage of the Muslim community is guilty of this evil. (Indeed, it is not only Muslims who suffer from our prejudice in the Middle East – Christians from the region are viewed with the same suspicion. If you are a Palestinian or an Iraqi, you are regarded as a security threat whatever your religion. Western unfamiliarity with Arabic names does not help. Two of my closest Christian friends from Iraq are called Osama and Jihad. These are everyday names where they come from, but in the West they set alarm bells ringing.) The remarks of Iran's president, Mahmoud Ahmadinejad, about Israel have further reinforced the idea that Islam, and especially Shia Islam, is essentially aggressive. Nothing could be further from the truth. The majority of Muslims in Iraq are Shia and I have found most of them to be peace-loving people.

This is not to deny the worldwide threat of al-Qa'ida. Today the danger it poses is real. Kenya, Tanzania, America, Indonesia, Spain, Britain, Algeria and Pakistan, if no others, have all suffered the consequences of its fundamentalist zeal. The result is that not only Islam but religion in general has gained a very bad name. So often when people in the West learn that I am a priest they start complaining about religion. They tell me that it is a major cause of most of the wars in the world today. I totally agree with them. They find this shocking, but I tell them that religion is like a hammer and chisel: it can be used either to create something beautiful or to cause total havoc. Too often it does the latter – as I point out when Christians tell me, as they often do, that what the world needs now is more religion. Sadly, when religion goes wrong, it really does go wrong. My job, however, is to try to make it go right. As I frequently tell people: If religion is part of the problem, it must be part of the solution.

I often watch Christian television when I am in Iraq. Most of it is American, and most of it shows a profound lack of understanding of what is happening in the wider world. Generally, it seems to be concerned only to make individuals feel good about themselves and to tell them how they can prosper financially. I find this hard to take when my people at St George's have nothing. There is no financial prosperity in store for them, and yet they are so sincere in their love for the Lord. On the other hand, I find great encouragement in channels such as the British-based God TV that have helped the FRRME so generously to help those who have nothing. I often say to Christians that we not only must pray for peace, we also must pay for peace. Too often we expect results to come not only quickly but cheaply. This is a point I am constantly making to governments and charitable trusts as well.

Demonizing Islam is not the only mistake we have

made in the West, however. We have misunderstood the very nature of this faith. When we talk of the need to 'strengthen the moderate Muslims' and deal only with them, who do we have in mind? Those Muslims who share our Western ideals. As a Christian and a priest, I would take great offence if I was called a 'moderate' believer. I am not. I am serious about my faith and my tradition. When I say the creed on Sundays, I mean it. And I share the concern of my Muslim brothers and sisters over the growing secularism and apostasy of Western society. True Islam, like true Christianity, is anything but moderate. Unfortunately, when we describe as 'moderates' those true Muslims who shun violence and abhor terrorism and are tolerant of 'the other', whether Christian or Jew, we only strengthen the position of those who do not and are not, and we encourage the view that it is they who are being true to their faith. I spend most of my time in the Middle East, and most of my colleagues are Muslims. Some of the people I trust most are Muslims – including those who translate for me now at church services. Not one of them is a moderate. They are ardently opposed to all forms of violence, but they are also extremely serious about their faith and their commitment to serving God. I have to say that I have more in common with them than I do with many of my so-called Christian colleagues.

If we genuinely want to resolve the very real problems between the West and the Islamic world, we need to begin by using the right language. In the first place, we have to abandon this talk of 'moderation'.

We need truly to respect Islam, which means having regard for those Muslims who are serious about their faith. In my experience, most Muslims are tolerant and ready to work with others, but they want other people to respect them, and even to be willing to learn from them. Indeed, it may well be that the West – and even the church – has a lot to learn from Islam. Perhaps we should begin by looking at ourselves and asking how we can become more serious about our beliefs. We should also disabuse ourselves of the idea that the best people to engage with Muslims are the liberal Christians. We need people in this field who are orthodox in their faith and committed. That is what Muslims expect all Christians to be.

Front-line peacemaking can be immensely stressful. This is not the kind of work where you can ask people to wait until another day. Often, your response has to be immediate, when a mosque or a church is blown up, a hostage is taken or a member of your staff is killed. On several occasions I have sat with my colleagues in Baghdad and cried at the news of a disaster or death we had tried to prevent. It has been an incredibly painful experience. However, there have also been times of immense joy. This is the nature of our work, put very simply. It is complex and intense and, for the present, much of it cannot be revealed, though one day I may be able to tell the full story. Searching for peace in the midst of violence is a risky business. It is so dangerous sometimes that very few people can do it. Nothing is certain about it – except that it has to be done. People must realize that it takes a very long time and we must not give up. Here in Iraq the work is often very solitary, very lonely and widely misunderstood. There are times when I wish I had a different calling. Then, suddenly, comes a small sign of progress: a Sunni and a Shia cleric share a meal together or a hostage is freed and, in a moment, hope is renewed.

This hope is often far more theological than political. Often Iraqi politics offers very little reason for optimism, but then unexpectedly the hope of the Resurrection breaks through. I think of days when all has seemed utterly bleak and I have gone in my mind to the empty tomb of Christ and just stood there. That empty tomb has been my inspiration. So, we take heart. The Spirit and the glory of God are here and, with the angels, are filling the atmosphere with the presence of the Lord. He is working in our world and I believe that the Middle East is at the centre of his purposes. The more I have worked in this region, the more I have come to see that it is God who is in control. I know that of myself I can do nothing but with God I can do everything. I have come to realize that what is happening in the physical realm is often just a manifestation of what is happening in the spiritual realm.

If you had asked me a few years ago what peacemaking boils down to, I would have given you a long and convoluted answer. Nowadays, I would simply say one word: love. It is love that leads us to forgiveness, which is the only thing that can prevent the pain of the past from dictating the future. Jesus taught us to love our enemies, but generally we do not even like them very much. So much of my time is spent with unpleasant people, and so before I approach them I simply pray: 'Lord, help me to love them!' If there is one passage in the Bible that is a prescription for my work, I would suggest it is Romans 12:9-21:

Love must be sincere. Hate what is evil; cling to what is good. Be devoted to one another in brotherly love. Honour one another above yourselves. Never be lacking in zeal, but keep your spiritual fervour, serving the Lord. Be joyful in hope, patient in affliction, faithful in prayer. Share with God's people who are in need. Practise hospitality.

Bless those who persecute you; bless and do not curse. Rejoice with those who rejoice; mourn with those who mourn. Live in harmony with one another. Do not be proud, but be willing to associate with people of low position. Do not be conceited.

Do not repay anyone evil for evil. Be careful to do what is right in the eyes of everybody. If it is possible, as far as it depends on you, live at peace with everyone. Do not take revenge, my friends, but leave room for God's wrath, for it is written: 'It is mine to avenge; I will repay,' says the Lord. On the contrary:

> *'If your enemy is hungry, feed him;*
> *if he is thirsty, give him something to drink.*
> *In doing this, you will heap burning coals*
> *on his head.'*

Do not be overcome by evil, but overcome evil with good.

There are times when it is very difficult to love, when you feel you have given so much and got nothing in return. Especially this is so in long-running hostage negotiations. Sometimes I feel angry as I make my way to a meeting, but I know that, if there is to be any prospect of progress, that anger must give way to love. In all my dealings with terrorists, it has been clear that they want something; but often I have had nothing to give them but love. This is in itself a form of sharing Jesus. So, we love, love and love and pray, pray and pray and hope, hope and hope that change will be brought about through the glory of God.

....

CHAPTER 7

The Most
Wonderful
Church in
the World

I T WAS ON MY EARLIEST TRIP to Iraq, in 1998,
that I first set eyes on the Anglican church of
St George of Mesopotamia. The Art Deco brick
building, which dates from 1936, was then rather
derelict, filthy and infested with pigeons – though the
stained-glass windows, adorned with various British
regimental crests, were all in good repair. No one had
worshipped in it for 14 years. A new caretaker had
lately been appointed, a former soldier called Hanna
who had spent 17 years as a prisoner of war in Iran,
but he had never been given any instructions. In fact,
though he was being paid $50 a month – more than
ten times what most Iraqis were earning – he seemed
to regard his job as part-time and spent most of his
day selling cigarettes. I showed him what he had to

do, and he immediately set to work. Within a matter of days he had transformed the church – from a dirty shell to a clean one. It didn't look very Anglican. Hanna is a Chaldean Catholic, and he had filled the building with plastic flowers, pictures of Mary and the smell of burning incense.

I said evening prayer in St George's most days during that first visit to Baghdad. The only other people in attendance were Hanna and the various members of the Mukhabarat who had been detailed to watch me. The church was a sad, sad place in those days. On my second visit to the country, I was accompanied by Colin Bennetts (then my bishop at Coventry), Peter Price (now Bishop of Bath and Wells, but then of Kingston) and Clive Handford, then Bishop of Cyprus and the Gulf, who had briefly been rector of St George's himself in 1967 and loved the place. I vividly remember the service in the church that Sunday, when the congregation consisted entirely of bishops, spies and the caretaker.

The years went by. Tariq Aziz, the Deputy Prime Minister under Saddam, gave me permission to take services there whenever I was in Baghdad, but every time I visited the church I wondered whether it would ever really function again. Apart from the Mukhabarat, my congregation was now made up mainly of United Nations staff. Hanna continued to look after the place. He got married to Rema, and they had a little girl named Mariam (Arabic for 'Mary'). Three years later, they had twin boys and called them Martin and George (after the church). After another two years, they had another boy and named him Andrew Clive after me and the bishop.

For five years, the church remained in disrepair. None of its outbuildings had doors or windows. Inside, they looked fit for nothing except to be pulled down. Really, there was no point in doing anything to them because they were so little used. As war loomed in 2003, I became increasingly anxious about Hanna and his family, who lived in the church hall. There were major government buildings around St George's – the Ministry of Information was its neighbour on one side and the National Theatre on the other – and I was very worried. I phoned Hanna and told him to take his family somewhere safer before the bombing started. He assured me that he would, but said that he himself had to stay behind at the church to look after it. Eventually I agreed to this, but I worried about him every day until the war was over.

When I returned to Iraq in May 2003, I was amazed to find that St George's was unscathed though the buildings on either side had been totally destroyed. Hanna, too, was in one piece, but in the chaos after the fall of Baghdad looters had broken into the church and tied him up while they stole everything except the marble font, the safe (which they had blown open) and, inexplicably left behind in it, a single cross of solid silver given in memory of a British soldier who had been killed in the First World War.

I will never forget the first service we held there after the liberation of Iraq. The congregation of about 50 consisted mostly of military personnel and diplomatic staff, though the Patriarch of the Ancient Church of the East (Old Calendar) turned up as well. The building was ringed with tanks and armoured personnel carriers, and helicopters clattered overhead like noisy angels. The security was so tight because there was reliable intelligence that someone was planning to blow the church up. I only learned this the next day, but apparently the Coalition people knew but came anyway. Canon Justin Welby, who was then co-director with me of Coventry's International Centre for Reconciliation, presided, and I preached from Haggai 2.9: "'The glory of this present house will be greater than the glory of the former house," says the LORD Almighty. "And in this place I will grant peace," declares the LORD Almighty.' The same verse, carved in stone, is set into one of the ruined walls of Coventry's old cathedral. I saw it almost every day when I was there and it expressed my hope for St George's. At that stage, I imagined that the 'greater glory of this house' would consist in the political changes for the better that we all expected to see. In fact, what followed was quite different.

Within weeks, the congregation became increasingly Iraqi. Soon the services had to be conducted in Arabic and my sermons were being translated by my assistant (and, by now, very close friend) Georges Sada. It wasn't long before almost 200 Iraqis were attending the church – though, as Baghdad outside the Green Zone descended deeper into darkness, all the Westerners stopped coming except one, the daughter of the British ambassador to Kuwait. Soon I appointed our first lay pastor, a fine man called Maher who as a convert from the Mandean faith had established his own evangelistic ministry. Whenever I was away, he did a wonderful job looking after the church and its congregation, while the services on Sundays were taken by my friend and colleague Colonel Frank Wismer, an Episcopalian who was chaplain to the Coalition Provisional Authority. By Christmas, we were regularly getting 300 people, including over a hundred children. With funding from the British Government and the Diocese of Cyprus and the Gulf, the doors and windows had been repaired, the brickwork cleaned inside and out and a carpet laid.

Even as St George's was coming to life, however, things were becoming more and more difficult for me. Merely getting there was hard work. I lived only two miles away but the roads were so congested that the journey through the heart of Baghdad could take as much as five hours each way. The traffic was terrible in the early days just after the war because so many people had celebrated their freedom by buying a new car. By the summer of 2004, however, it was hard to get petrol, and drivers would queue for two days or more just to fill up their tanks. After a while, I moved to a house by the Tigris, on the other side of town. My new home was twice as far from the church, but because we no longer had to drive through the city centre it never took more than an hour to get there.

The congregation at St George's continued to grow steadily, and in the space of a few months the outbuildings which I had thought were beyond hope were beautifully restored. In April 2005, however, we had very bad news. Maher and his wife and their 14-year-old son had gone to a Christian conference in Jordan, accompanied by his assistant. On their way home, they rang me on a satellite phone as they crossed the border back into Iraq – and that was the last we ever heard of them. Neither they nor their driver, nor three others in their party, were ever seen again. It seems likely that they were abducted and killed – many people were being kidnapped at the time – but we never received a ransom demand. I appointed a temporary replacement for Maher while we waited in vain for news of him. We also had to take care of his surviving child, a teenage girl.

In all, 11 of my staff were killed or disappeared that year. Eventually, the British ambassador decided that it was too dangerous for me to live outside the Green Zone and so I moved inside its fortifications, from my lovely, nine-bedroomed, riverside house to a new address: 27 Foss Way, Ocean Cliffs, Baghdad. There were no cliffs, however, and certainly no view. My new home was a small plastic trailer in an underground car park. It was not en-suite, so I had to use the public 'rest rooms'. (Bizarrely, these were all named after Oxford and Cambridge colleges. Of course, I went first to the room named after my old college, Clare, but I found it was for women only. The one next door was named after All Souls College, Oxford, but someone had crossed that out and written 'Trent Polytechnic' instead – a much less august establishment, but rather more appropriate.)

In the end, I was told it was too dangerous for me even to go to St George's. Indeed, it was dangerous for the congregation to go there, and so from then on they came into the shelter of the Green Zone every week. We held our services in either the Prime Minister's office or that of my friend and colleague Dr Mowaffak, and there we would worship for hours at a time in freedom and safety. The children came in their hordes along with their mothers and the few fathers who were still alive. I am sure we were the only church in the world that met in the office of a Shia Muslim, and I often described this as interfaith relations at the cutting edge. Most of the security men who guarded these premises were South Americans, and being good Catholics they loved to join us for Communion – and we loved to have them with us. Sometimes I was able to get one of the American military chaplains to come and preach, and I often conducted baptisms with a red plastic washing-up bowl.

One disappointment we had was when the father of Philip Rizk, then the FRRME's man in Gaza, sent us a load of illustrated children's Bibles and the truck that was bringing them was stolen en route to Iraq. We had plenty of Bibles for adults, but none for the children. A few months later, we were holding a service in Dr Mowaffak's office when a man called Ali came in. '*Abuna* ['Father'],' he said to me, 'you never told me all the children come here.' Of course I hadn't: Ali is a senior member of the Mehdi Army. However, he left the room and five minutes later returned with dozens of children's Bibles. I looked inside them and saw they were the very ones that had been stolen. They might not have reached us by the route we intended, but by God's grace they had got to us nonetheless. The children were delighted.

One of them, a six-year-old girl called Vivian, was ill – we were told she had bladder cancer, probably caused by uranium dust. On one occasion when I prayed for her, her father told me that the radiotherapy machine at the hospital was no longer working. I remember very clearly laying hands on her and asking God not that she would be healed but that we would find the right doctor to treat her. That night, I prayed for her for three hours or so. The next day, I was preaching at an evangelical service in the Palace. When it was over, I stood at the door of the chapel saying 'Goodbye, General. Goodbye, Colonel' when suddenly I saw an officer I had not met before. I got talking to him and it turned out that Major Gibbons was born just a few miles from where I live in Hampshire. I asked what he was doing in Baghdad, and he told me he was working at 'the Cash' (the combat support hospital).

I asked him what he did there and he said: 'Oh, I'm just a urologist.' I could have kissed him. 'Just a urologist!' I said. 'You are the one man in the world I needed to meet right now.' I told him all about Vivian and he asked me to bring her to the hospital the next day. It proved to be very difficult to get her in, but with the help of the command surgeon, who was a member of my Anglican congregation in the Palace, we succeeded. It was clear that Vivian's situation was serious: the cancer was developing and her bladder had to be removed. There was no one who could do the operation in Iraq. Major Gibbons investigated the possibility of getting it done in America, but none of the little girl's family spoke any English and that was a problem. Finally, he found a surgeon in Jordan who had trained in America and had specialized in Vivian's form of cancer. This man agreed to treat her at the King Hussein Cancer Hospital in Amman.

I had a week to find about £30,000 to pay for all this involved, which I managed to do – not least with the help of the Anglican congregation in the Palace. We took Vivian and her father to Jordan, where I discussed her extensive treatment and her prospects with the surgeon while she underwent the preliminary chemotherapy. Eventually, it was time for the operation and Vivian had her entire bladder removed. She endured the pain so well! Afterwards, her mother and her brothers were able to join her and we moved the whole family into a house. The day she came out of hospital was a day of great celebration.

I told her I would get her anything she wanted, and it turned out there were two things: a doll from England and a mobile. When we gave them to her, she was so happy! She made very good progress. Fortunately, my former colleague Fadel Alfatlawi, who used to run the IIP, was now in Jordan and he took responsibility for Vivian's family and did a great job. She continued to get better, and it was a joy to see her playing and dancing again. One day, Fadel told her that when she grew up he would marry her. She informed him that that was impossible, as she was going to marry Father Andrew.

Every day, whether I was in Iraq or Britain, I would phone to find out how Vivian was. The news was always good until one day I was told she couldn't see out of her left eye. It was a dreadful blow. I spoke to her doctor and it was apparent that she had a secondary tumour on her optic nerve and there was now nothing more that could be done. When Vivian came home from hospital, she was dying. I had hoped so much and prayed so much for this child, whom I loved like one of my own. All around the world, people were praying for her – Christians, Muslims and Jews – yet as I was leaving for Britain at the beginning of April 2007 I kissed her goodbye and knew I would not see her alive again. I said the prayer that the old priest Simeon had said when he saw the infant Jesus: 'Lettest now thy servant depart in peace, for my eyes have seen the glory of my salvation.' I flew back home with a very heavy heart. I thought about Major Gibbons, how we had met, how God had surely been involved. I didn't know why Vivian should now be dying but I knew she was in the care of Jesus. She told her parents that angels kept coming to see her, and I knew it would not be long before she went to live with them.

One night, Fadel phoned me to say that Vivian was in a coma in hospital, where he and her father were with her. The next day, I was due to fly to America to speak at a healing conference led by the televangelist Benny Hinn, but as I was packing my bags early that morning Fadel rang me to say that Vivian had died. I cried as I cannot remember ever crying before. I told my staff I would not be going to America after all, but back to Jordan to take her funeral the next day. It was to be the hardest funeral I had ever taken, but it was also a day of celebration for a beautiful little girl. I told the congregation that she was so wonderful that Jesus needed her. Vivian, my Vivian, was in heaven. I went back to Baghdad and told her relations and friends and all the people of St George's about the service. All of us had tears in our eyes as we celebrated her life together. Her immediate family remained in Jordan until September 2008, when they were granted permission to emigrate to France. I am sure I will see them again, and I will not stop loving them all.

By the start of 2007, the congregation numbered well over a thousand and there was nowhere in the Green Zone large enough to fit everyone in. The violence was starting to abate a little, and I began once more to hold services in the church – though I had to be escorted there by five heavily-armed bodyguards from GardaWorld. I hadn't seen St George's for over a year. We furnished each of our people with a photocard so that we could regularly give them food and money. Their needs are immense, and if we do not give, they do not have. The cost of this provision is colossal and is met primarily by British churches. We also provide food for people who live in the neighbourhood – most of whom are Muslims – as well as for several institutions in Baghdad that help the sick, the elderly and the disabled. Not least is our commitment to the Mother Teresa Home for children born with serious disabilities, which is a particular concern of our Mothers' Union.

I'm often asked about the Mothers' Union in Baghdad, what it does and why it was set up. Worldwide, the MU is the largest missionary organization in the Anglican Church. As none of my congregation was originally Anglican, I decided that it was important to enhance our Anglican identity in some way. This our Mothers' Union has truly achieved. We launched it on Easter Day 2006 and we now have by far the largest branch in the Middle East. Led by Nawal, the wife of our lay pastor Faiz, the MU is now the biggest group in the church, with over a thousand members. They wear their badges proudly and are at the forefront of our relief work, providing food and making clothes and curtains and other essentials for people's homes. Their room in the church is equipped with several sewing machines and they also have their own kitchen. They meet several times a week to pray and study together, and they work so hard for the whole community.

By the beginning of 2007 we had two lay pastors, Faiz and Majid, both wonderful men of God. One day, I was at home in sleepy Hampshire, walking down my road, when I got a phone call from my young friend David, who lives and works at the church. 'They've kidnapped Majid!' he shouted. I took a big breath and said I would phone Samir in Iraq. It was obvious from the information we had gathered that Majid's abductors were seeking financial gain rather than political advantage, which was actually very good news. I told my staff to find out how much they wanted. The answer was $60,000. The church didn't have that much – but that very morning we received a large gift of £20,000 from God TV and so we were able to make an offer of $40,000, which was accepted. Majid was returned amid great rejoicing. He told us that throughout his ordeal he had kept praying out loud and quoting scripture, and when his kidnappers had asked him why, he had told them. Their ringleader said that usually they killed their victims but for some unknown reason they couldn't kill him. However, they assured him that they would if he or his family returned to his house, even to collect their clothes, and so he and his wife and children had to move into St George's. It soon became obvious that it was not safe for them even to remain in Iraq and so very sadly we said farewell to them and sent them to Syria.

St George's stands in Haifa Street, which is now one of the most dangerous in Baghdad. In the first few days of 2007, there was a big gun battle there between a number of different groups, including the Mehdi Army and al-Qa'ida. Many people were killed, and when I next came down the street on my way to church I saw 50 or 60 bodies hanging from the trees and lamp posts. Every week, I ask my congregation what they want to tell me and people say, 'I went to the market and someone next to me was shot dead' or 'A car bomb went off and I just managed to escape.' All but a handful of the men have been killed, and a lot of the women dress in black because they are mourning the loss of a loved one. In July 2007, I told the US Commission on International Religious Freedom that 'in the past month 36 of my own congregation have been kidnapped. To date, only one has been returned.'

In the first five months of 2008, another 89 were taken or killed. Usually, we are never told why.

In May 2007, after four of its security men were kidnapped, GardaWorld announced that its employees would no longer venture outside the Green Zone. Thankfully, Dr Mowaffak again proved his friendship and nowadays I am escorted to and from St George's by at least 25 men of the Iraqi special forces from his own personal detail. My GardaWorld bodyguards drive me from my trailer to Dr Mowaffak's compound nearby and there, encased in body armour, I take my seat in an armour-plated car with blackened windows. Surrounded by military vehicles, we proceed slowly, stopping at countless checkpoints. When we finally leave the Green Zone, we are met by a convoy of police cars and more military vehicles and now we drive at speed, with sirens blaring and guns pointed out of the windows. If we encounter a traffic jam, the other drivers are ordered through loudspeakers to clear the road. If that doesn't do the trick, our whole convoy simply moves to the wrong side of the road – still at speed. At every crossroads, the police have stopped all the traffic. When we arrive at St George's, the street is closed off. Soldiers run to surround the building while others check inside to make sure it is safe. Only then am I finally allowed to get out of the car, to be met by scores of our children. I never dreamed I would ever go to church like this – but then again I never thought my parish would be in Baghdad.

Despite these pressures, St George's in 2007 was very full and very alive. The congregation still sat on the white plastic garden chairs we had bought after the war, but the worship was out of this world. Every week I fell more deeply in love with this church and all its people. Faiz and Nawal were inspiring. By the end of that year the congregation had grown so large we couldn't fit everyone in at one sitting, so we began to hold two services, one on Saturdays (following the custom of Christians in the Middle East) and one on Sundays (which is a weekday in Iraq – but as most of our people do not have jobs, this is no problem). Once again, God TV came to our rescue and paid for pews for the whole church. These are quite splendid, but already they are not enough for the numbers who come and so the garden chairs are back as well – and still people have to sit on the floor or stand, while we worship as I have never worshipped before.

People often ask me what the services are like at this special church, but they are hard to describe. In Britain, a vicar would usually impose his or her own style on their church, but in Baghdad my people impose their style on me and it is simply wonderful. It is a mix of Orthodox, Catholic and charismatic (which I suppose is essentially rather Anglican). We have pictures of the saints that the people kiss as they come in, and they dip their hands in the font and cross themselves. Everyone stands to pray, with their hands held out in front of them, and there is much bowing. We conduct our services largely in Arabic, with the most important prayers in Aramaic, the language of Jesus. I know enough of both to say the liturgy, though I have to preach in English and pause while my words are translated.

I make my sermons very culturally relevant – I always talk about what has happened locally and recently. I talk about the saints, and especially those these people really revere: Mariam, Jona, 'doubting' Toma and the church's patron saint, Gorgis. The people are very serious about their own, individual relationships to God, but they have told me lately that they have learned so much from us and how we explain the Bible to them, almost as though that was never done before. We have just started doing the Alpha course at St George's, which is a basic introduction to Christianity – I've been doing it at the Palace with Coalition personnel since March 2004 – and over 800 of my people have signed up for it.

I also talk a lot about Iraq in the Bible, where it is referred to as 'the land of Shinar' or as 'Mesopotamia' (which means 'between the rivers', Tigris and Euphrates), or by the name of one of its greatest cities, Babylon. I tell them that the Garden of Eden was here, and the tower of Babel; that Noah built the Ark here; that Abraham came from Ur and Isaac's wife Rebekah from Nahor (where Jacob met his wives-to-be Leah and Rachel), which are both in present-day Iraq; that Jonah went as an evangelist to Nineveh, on the edge of modern-day Mosul, and so did Thomas on his way to India; that Daniel survived the lions' den here and Shadrach, Meshach and Abednego met the Son of God in the fiery furnace here; that Esther was queen here; that Amos and Ezekiel prophesied here, Belshazzar saw the writing on the wall here, the Magi came from

here and Peter preached here. In fact, Israel/Palestine
is the only land that is mentioned more frequently in
the Bible.

We have a full robed choir and there is a
great deal of energetic and enthusiastic singing,
accompanied by an electric piano (the church organ
was stolen long ago). There is no set length for our
services, though people have to get home before it
is dark and sometimes the soldiers have to hurry me
away for security reasons. Many of the songs we use
are songs well known in Western churches translated
into Arabic; but too often the sentiments these express
are irrelevant to the situation here in Baghdad and so
I have written some new ones. One of these appears at
the end of this book.

Of all our services, I especially love the children's
first communions. They all wear lovely white robes
made for them by the Mothers' Union and process
into the church singing. At a recent first communion,
two of the children – one aged ten, the other eight –
were in tears as they walked up the aisle. I took them
aside and asked them why they were crying. They told
me: 'This is the most important day of our lives and as
we were walking in, Jesus was with us.'

At the beginning of our services, I declare: *Allah
hu ma'na* ('God is here'). The congregation reply: *Wa
Ruh al-Qudus ma'na aithan* ('And his Holy Spirit is here').
This is how most Anglican services around the world
begin; but when you have lost everything, as these
people have, you realize that Jesus is all you have
left. Recently, I spent two days speaking at a small

conference for Episcopalian US Army chaplains in
Iraq and I introduced them to some of their fellow
Christians from St George's. The man who organized
the conference, Colonel Dale Marta, sent this report
to his bishop:

> *The meeting with Canon White and members*
> *of his congregation ... was a profound spiritual*
> *experience for me. I will never be quite the same.*
> *In the loud rushing wind of media and politics*
> *that swirls around Iraq, I heard the small still*
> *voice through the humble and precious people of*
> *St George's and her spiritual leader. I no longer*
> *can hide in the safety of the cave but feel driven to*
> *stay engaged with Iraq and her people through St*
> *George's.*

At that meeting, one of the chaplains asked what was
so special about our church. Everybody replied with
the same answer: love. We not only talk about love,
we practise it. We love our Lord and Master, we love
each other – and I love my people and they love me. I
never thought I would love my congregation as I do.
I never thought I would be loved by my congregation
as I am. We are surrounded by violence and the tools
of violence, but when we come to church we come
to worship and to love. There is a lot of laughter –
sometimes at my expense! – as well as tears.

The fact is that we have the biggest Christian
congregation in Iraq. Currently, it is growing at a rate
of a hundred a month and it now numbers 1,800,

including 500 children. Apart from me there are no real Anglicans in St George's, and yet everyone is so committed to it. They used to go to the Chaldean churches, or the Assyrian, Armenian or Latin Catholic churches. In fact, the other priests are really cross with me because my congregation is huge and now they have nobody. I feel bad about this, but I didn't exactly go sheep-stealing – these people came to St George's because either they lived near the church or they had heard good things about it. At first, I said I hoped that once the violence had stopped, people would go back to their own churches; but if anyone mentions this nowadays, everyone insists that this is their church and they will never leave it. (It's not an easy issue. Many of Iraq's old churches are threatened by new arrivals. A host of foreign missionaries showed up after the war in 2003, and today there are 12 new evangelical churches in Baghdad. This is a serious disturbance of the status quo. People want freedom of religion – but not too much!)

In June 2008, the new bishop of Cyprus and the Gulf, Michael Lewis, visited Iraq. Everyone was so excited to see him, and he was greeted like a patriarch. One of his duties was to open our new medical and dental clinic. The kidnappers in Iraq had targeted professionals in particular, and by now over 80 per cent of Baghdad's doctors had either been killed or fled the country. As a result, it had become very difficult for people to get treatment. So, we set up a free clinic with funding from the US Army, with three doctors and three dentists – one of them Jewish – all from the neighbourhood. Now, people come to church for the good of their bodies as well as their spirits. Most of our patients are not even Christians, let alone members of our congregation, but it is to the church they come for help and there is no discrimination. Thus St George's not only provides opportunity to worship the Almighty, it also meets people's physical needs. One week we give everyone food, the next we give them money. Sceptics may say that this is why our congregation is so large, and I have wondered that as well – but the people themselves insist: Even if you gave us nothing we would still come for the love.

I can't pretend that there are never any problems within the church, but they are always very minor. Among the teenagers there is a lot of jealousy over whom I love the most. If I rang one person and not another, word would soon go round that *Abuna* had favoured so-and-so. Even as I write this, I have just had a phone call from one of our young people telling me that someone else wants to call me daddy and I mustn't let her. I explained that we must love everybody and after a while I think they got the message.

In the summer of 2008, six of the young people from St George's were able to come to Britain with me. Three of them stayed at my house in Hampshire, and three at the home of some local friends, Robert and Tanya, who have a swimming pool, a tennis court, a lake and a large collection of vintage cars. They had a wonderful time. They travelled around the country – in Oxfordshire they were given lunch by Nina Prentice, the wife of the current British ambassador to Iraq. They even spent two days at the House of Lords with the chair of the FRRME, Lord Hylton, our patron, Lord Carey, and the former Leader of the Lords, Baroness Amos, whose father taught me (and inspired me) when I was at school. When they returned with me to Baghdad, one of these young people said to me: 'You took us to heaven. Now we are back in hell.' I told him that one day Iraq will be heaven again. After all, the Garden of Eden was in Mesopotamia. Paradise it once was, and paradise I believe it will be again one day.

At the beginning of 2008, some of my supporters complained that the updates I was sending out devoted too much space to St George's. It was true – but that was because at the time the church was my only source of hope and encouragement. To me, it is simply the most wonderful church in the world. I love all my people, and though Baghdad is the most dangerous place on earth I have no desire ever to leave. My mind goes back to my first sermon here after the war, on Haggai 2.9: 'The glory of this present house will be greater than the glory of the former house ... and in this place I will grant peace.' I never dreamed how that promise would be fulfilled in this church, but as I reflect on that verse it strikes me that today St George's is filled with the glory of the Lord and, even though there is violence all around, it is a place of the profoundest peace.

CHAPTER 8

··

The
Kingdom,
the Power
and the
Glory

I T MAY SOUND WONDERFUL practising one's ministry in the corridors of power, but I spend most of my time in much more dangerous places. I have been beaten, held at gunpoint, left for hours in rat-infested rooms and much more besides. On one occasion, I was even locked in a room whose floor was littered with human fingers and toes. I didn't know whether I was next to be maimed. I was fortunate I was not. In addition to all this, my health is not good – I constantly feel enervated, my balance gets progressively worse and at times my speech is slurred and my sight is very poor. Many people would like to see me put out to grass. Almost every day, people ask me how I manage to keep going.

I remember not so long ago contemplating my job while I was sitting waiting for a military helicopter in the Green Zone. When you fly in one of these machines, there is no safety briefing. The doors are left wide open and soldiers lean out with their guns trained on the ground. Usually you are shot at, which takes a little getting used to. I thought of the days when I used to cycle round my old parish in London – now even the ride along the busy South Circular Road seemed utterly serene. I recalled my time at theological college and what I learned there. They didn't teach me to write a *fatwa* for Islamic clerics or to negotiate for the release of hostages, but they did teach me theology and they gave me the tools to understand the scriptures. I took out my Bible and it suddenly struck me that even this looked different. It wasn't bound in beautiful black leather, its pages were not edged with gold. Instead, it was khaki-coloured and its cover said '3rd Squadron of the 7th Cavalry Regiment'. It was an American military Bible. Nonetheless, it contained the same words that keep me going each day. I opened it to Psalm 62 and read verse 2: 'He only is my rock and my salvation, my stronghold; I shall not be greatly shaken' (NASB). Yes, I am surrounded by trouble, but my God, the God of Abraham, Isaac and Jacob, does not change, for he is my rock. He sustains me even when everything seems to be going against me.

This is the most vital aspect of my work: that everything I do is underpinned by my faith. Much of the church today has rejected the word 'religion' and I agree with a lot of what has been said on this subject, but I also believe strongly that there is a crucial meaning in the Latin root of that word: *ligare*, to bind. I am bound to my God as he is revealed in Jesus Christ, who is my Master, my Leader and my Messiah. I rely on him completely in my work. I could not attempt to do it without him. It is fine to have debates and sermons on the danger of 'the spirit of religion', but here in the midst of conflict that is not our concern. Our priority is doing the work of the Kingdom of God, enabling his rule to come to earth. The more you are surrounded by violence and bloodshed, the more you have to rely on the love of God and the direction of his Holy Spirit. The more you recognize your own inadequacy, the more you realize that nothing can be achieved unless you trust and hope simply in God.

The following is an account I wrote for my supporters of a recent Sunday in Baghdad. It shows the true nature of my work in Iraq. It also shows the true nature of God, our rock and salvation.

Do you ever have days when you know that God's glory is going to come? Well, today was one of those days. I started on Saturday night with my security team. 'Tomorrow is a God day, not a political day.' 'Yes, sir' was the reply.

Early in the morning we made our way to the Prime Minister's offices. Not for politics but for God. It has been decided that it is far too dangerous for me to go to St George's, so we had the service in the Prime Minister's lecture theatre at his

*invitation. It took the congregation over two hours
to enter because of security. ...*

*I chose as my text just three words from one
of the letters of John: 'God is love.' We had a
wonderful service: great singing, OK preaching
and tears ... What was clear was that it is only the
love of Jesus that sustains these wonderful people at
such a difficult time. ...*

*We then had Holy Communion and as we broke
bread God's glory came. I cannot explain why or
what happened, but our Lord was there in power.
We then baptized a young child, just 17 days old,
called Alexandria. Once again there was great joy,
joy that God loved this little girl and us.*

*From the Prime Minister's office we went at
full speed to the Palace for the service there. As we
arrived, mortar [bombs] came over. The soldiers
made us dive for cover and for a short while
nobody was allowed into the Palace. I was actually
quite grateful for this, because I was late...*

*Here I am doing a series on people in the
Bible who dwelt in Iraq. Today it was the turn of
Ezekiel. I spoke of the glory that he saw, I spoke
of God's glory that I have seen here, glory like no
other place. I told people to expect to see God's
glory here. I read them part of a recent e-mail from
Brett, Alyssa and Emily from All Nations Church
in Charlotte, North Carolina. People saw that if
these young people can experience the glory of God,
surely they could as well.*

As I celebrated Holy Communion, God's glory

*came again. As I looked down from the altar I
could see military officers, with their guns beside
them, in tears. Tough men with big tears. After the
service, person after person came and said they had
seen God's glory in the service. They stayed by me,
and we had lunch together and talked more of the
glory of God. ...*

*In the evening [session of our Alpha course,] we
dealt with the subject of how we can be sure of our
faith. I spoke from 2 Corinthians 5. Once again
I read out the e-mail from the girls of All Nations
Church as a perfect example of being able to
experience God's love. Once again this was a truly
glorious session when the Lord was very present.
Literally everybody said it was amazing. ...*

*So, this was a Sunday in Baghdad, a day
when God's glory again broke forth. I know more
now than ever that all things are in the hands
of God and he decides. He is indeed our rock
and salvation. As I left my security team tonight,
they said, 'Today was very different. Something
happened to us!'*

*When we meet with God, we see not only his
glory, we see that he is unmoving, unchanging and
all-sustaining. Without him there is no hope and
no future. ... This is my God, this is my rock, which
enables me to continue the work of the Almighty
come what may. All may change but my God is the
same yesterday, today and forever. I say again: he is
my rock, my strength, my salvation and my fortress
in times of trouble.*

People ask me why I spend so much time in places such as Gaza and Baghdad. The truth is, because that is where I am sent. And so I am never afraid. Some people say that it is the very fact that I have no fear that puts my life in particular danger; but the reason I am not afraid is because I have an uncomplicated, almost childlike faith in God. Every night, I begin my prayers in the same way that I did as a boy. Maybe this is why I love and care for children so much. It is in their faces that we can see the face of Jesus in a simple, wholesome way. The more I have done this type of work, and the more I have struggled with the reality of death and destruction, the more I have had to put my trust simply in my Lord and my God. My faith has grown, and I no longer experience my spiritual highs only when I am in a wonderful church service. Now it is a matter of seeing the glory of God wherever I find myself. All that is needed is awareness. Each day I ask God to come with me on my difficult journey and each day I see his glory at work. It is that that sustains me, along with the friendship and support of my colleagues.

Many people are astonished when I say that the people I am closest to in my work are not Christians at all. One is a Jew and the other a Muslim: Rabbi Michael Melchior and Dr Mowaffak al-Rubaie. Both are fine politicians, and both are men of great faith. I consider them to be nothing less than a gift from God. When I say this in public meetings, people are often not just amazed but indignant. They ask: How can my most vital allies be followers of other faiths? I have to insist that the God I serve is not a Christian either. He is the God of Abraham, Isaac and Jacob. Others who have met Rabbi Melchior and Dr Mowaffak have told me that they, too, have seen God in them. My audiences are often surprised, but then my God is the God of surprises.

However, though I work predominantly with people of other faiths, it does not mean that my own faith has in any way been diluted. In fact, it is stronger now than ever. I give thanks to God that I have never doubted him. He is indeed for me 'the same yesterday, today and forever'. However dreadful the tragedy, my Lord is there. Amidst the greatest havoc I have witnessed in post-war Iraq or in Gaza, or in Bethlehem during the siege, I have still seen his glory – the same glory I saw in the worship at St Mark's, Kennington and at All Nations Church in Charlotte, and in the life and ministry of Sister Ruth Heflin. I have seen the heavens opened and glimpsed something of the majesty, might and love of God.

When life is full of despair, it is only the glory of God that truly sustains. There have been times when everything has gone wrong, when friends and colleagues have been killed and there has seemed to be no hope. It is at times like this that I ask God to show me his glory. He always does so, though sometimes I do not see it immediately. It has been manifested as a mighty cloud over Baghdad, and on one memorable occasion I have sensed it in the singing of a hymn one Easter morning when the birds were singing and the bombs were going off. God is here, and his Spirit is with us! When one is in the glory of God, miraculous things can happen and one is no longer restricted by the life of humanity. So, as I circulate among the powerful people in the Pentagon, Congress and Parliament, I ask to see God's glory and in all these places I have seen it. It is when the power and the glory come together that we witness change. That is why I say that my work is about the power and the glory – the power of those who run this world and the glory of the God who runs the universe. For too long people have tried to keep them separate, but God is at work in time and space and they have to be brought together.

When I am sitting in my little trailer in Baghdad, or being bundled from one meeting to another, it is not easy to stay abreast of what is happening in the wider world. Often, people ask me for my opinion on the way the world is going – on globalization, climate change, the growing dominance of China. The truth is that I have nothing to say about these issues. I do not have time even to think about them. To me, they seem to be things that preoccupy people who live in peace and comfort. The questions that plague me are much more immediate. When will the next rocket come? Am I well enough to get to the bunker outside if the barrage starts up again? Have we got enough money for the ransom if I am abducted? Have we got enough money to feed the people of St George's this month? The challenge for us is simple: to survive today. Though I can honestly say I have never been anxious for myself,

I do worry about my congregation. I worry, too, about friends like Dr Mowaffak.

Amidst these concerns, I stop and turn to God. I am drawn back to the words that end Isaiah 19:

> *In that day there will be a highway from Egypt to Assyria. The Assyrians will go to Egypt and the Egyptians to Assyria. The Egyptians and Assyrians will worship together. In that day Israel will be the third, along with Egypt and Assyria, a blessing on the earth. The Lord Almighty will bless them, saying, 'Blessed be Egypt my people, Assyria my handiwork, and Israel my inheritance.'*

Egypt, Assyria – that is, Iraq – and Israel are all places where I work, and I have a profound sense that in the midst of all this conflict the Lord is here and his Spirit is with us. All my hope for this broken world rests in God. And it is a huge hope, a hope I find in scripture and also in hymns. There are four hymns in particular that have had profound meaning for me in the Middle East. Every day I listen to them and every day I reflect on their words. Each one has its own story.

Because He Lives
GLORIA AND WILLIAM GAITHER, 1971

It was Maundy Thursday, 2005. I had to speak at an Easter sunrise service beside Saddam's old swimming pool in Baghdad and I was struggling to find a suitable text. Before I went to sleep, I prayed that God would speak to me and direct me what to say – and in the middle of the night I woke up with a song going through my head. I hadn't sung it since I was a child at Sunday school.

These are the words:

God sent his Son – they called him Jesus,
He came to love, heal and forgive;
He lived and died to buy my pardon,
An empty grave is there to prove my Saviour lives.

Because he lives, I can face tomorrow,
Because he lives, all fear is gone;
Because I know he holds the future
And life is worth the living just because he lives.

How sweet to hold a newborn baby
And feel the pride and joy he gives;
But greater still the calm assurance:
This child can face uncertain days because
he lives.

And then one day I'll cross the river,
I'll fight life's final war with pain;
And then, as death gives way to vict'ry,
I'll see the lights of glory and I'll know he reigns.

There was no doubt that this was to be my message. It was a difficult time and things looked very black. Everyone was wondering what we were doing in Iraq

174

at all. We sang this hymn and the final verse spoke deeply to so many of us that day and gave us hope. It also confronted me and others, with an apocalyptic question: Could this indeed be it, the end of the world, life's absolutely 'final war with pain'? And if so, would we see indeed death 'giving way to victory'?

A few weeks later, I was visiting Wheaton College, near Chicago, when my mobile phone rang. It was a woman I didn't know. She told me her name was Gloria and she had written that hymn. It was a truly wonderful encounter. It wasn't long before I went to see her and her husband, Bill Gaither. I heard the story that inspired her words, about their newborn son and the pain that Gloria was suffering at the time. Her sentiments had uplifted us 34 years later at Easter in Baghdad.

God Will Take Care of You
CIVILLA D MARTIN, 1904

The second hymn did not impact me until late in 2007. We didn't have a pianist at the time for the Anglican services in the Palace, so one of the soldiers in the congregation played her flute and she also chose the hymns. When we came to the end of the service, the hymn she had selected brought tears to my eyes. Once again, I hadn't sung it since I was a boy. It was, again, a bad time. Rockets were pounding into the Green Zone, and though the surge was well under way, things did not seem to be going well at the time.

Our only assurance was that, despite everything, God would take care of us.

> *Be not dismayed whate'er betide,*
> *God will take care of you;*
> *Beneath his wings of love abide,*
> *God will take care of you.*

> *God will take care of you,*
> *Through every day, o'er all the way;*
> *He will take care of you,*
> *God will take care of you.*

We came to the second verse:

> *Through days of toil when heart doth fail,*
> *God will take care of you;*
> *When dangers fierce your path assail,*
> *God will take care of you.*

Without question, these words applied to all of us. Every week at St George's, I tell my people that I cannot assure any of them that they – or I – will not be killed; but what I can guarantee them is that we shall all meet again in heaven, and when we see Jesus we shall be like him.

> *All you may need he will provide,*
> *God will take care of you;*
> *Nothing you ask will be denied,*
> *God will take care of you.*

No matter what may be the test,
God will take care of you;
Lean, weary one, upon his breast,
God will take care of you.

Never Alone

LUDIE D PICKETT, 1897

In May 2008, the Green Zone was coming under rocket attack at least 40 times a day. It was rather funny, because every time a rocket landed I would be phoned by members of St George's wanting to know that I was all right. One evening, I was preaching at the evangelical service in the Palace when the sirens started to blare. We were singing a hymn at the time that I had never heard before. Everyone apart from Samir and I got down on the floor. Even the pianist was on the floor, but he managed to keep on playing and so we kept on singing:

I've seen the lightning flashing,
I've heard the thunder roll.
I've felt sin's breakers dashing,
Which almost conquered my soul.
I've heard the voice of my Saviour,
Bidding me still to fight on.
He promised never to leave me,
Never to leave me alone!

No, never alone, no never alone,
He promised never to leave me,

He'll claim me for his own;
No, never alone, no never alone.
He promised never to leave me,
Never to leave me alone.

The world's fierce winds are blowing,
Temptation sharp and keen.
I have a peace in knowing
My Saviour stands between –
He stands to shield me from danger
When my friends are all gone.
He promised never to leave me,
Never to leave me alone!

When in affliction's valley
I tread the road of care,
My Saviour helps me carry
The cross so heavy to bear;
Though all around me is darkness,
Earthly joys all flown;
My Saviour whispers his promise,
Never to leave me alone!

He died on Calvary's mountain,
For me they pierced his side.
For me he opened that fountain,
The crimson, cleansing tide.
For me he waiteth in glory,
Seated upon his throne.
He promised never to leave me,
Never to leave me alone!

'Fierce winds' were certainly blowing in Baghdad, and the danger was very real; but we trusted in a God who would never leave us, who always stood to shield us. Truly, we are never alone.

Just As I Am Without One Plea
CHARLOTTE ELLIOTT, 1835

The latest hymn to inspire me is the one I know best.

Just as I am, without one plea,
But that thy blood was shed for me,
And that thou bidst me come to thee,
O Lamb of God, I come, I come.

I have sung it so many times, but now in Iraq it suddenly means so much more. One of my very closest friends is the evangelist J John. We often go away together, and he is the only person who phones me even in Baghdad. I get his e-mailed newsletters every Monday, and in one of them he wrote about Charlotte Elliott, the writer of this hymn, and how she was challenged to come to true faith. I was amazed to read that she came from the corner of south London where I was once a minister. I was even more surprised when this hymn was chosen to end our service the following Sunday in the chapel in the Palace.

Just as I am, and waiting not
To rid my soul of one dark blot,

To thee whose blood can cleanse each spot,
O Lamb of God, I come, I come.

Just as I am, though tossed about
With many a conflict, many a doubt,
Fightings and fears within, without,
O Lamb of God, I come, I come.

Just as I am, poor, wretched, blind;
Sight, riches, healing of the mind,
Yea, all I need in thee to find,
O Lamb of God, I come, I come.

Just as I am, thou wilt receive,
Wilt welcome, pardon, cleanse, relieve;
Because thy promise I believe,
O Lamb of God, I come, I come.

Just as I am, thy love unknown
Hath broken every barrier down;
Now, to be thine, yea, thine alone,
O Lamb of God, I come, I come.

Just as I am, of that free love
The breadth, length, depth and height to prove,
Here for a season, then above,
O Lamb of God, I come, I come!

Every verse inspires me, but it is the third that speaks to
me most deeply. Truly, in Baghdad we are 'tossed about
with many a conflict' – though I have to confess that I

haven't experienced 'many a doubt'. I have never for even one moment doubted the power and love of my God. I realize that this makes me unusual, but maybe that is why God has sent me to Iraq. Though I spend much of my time meeting some of the most powerful people in the world, and seem always to be involved in very serious conversations, my trust in God is very simple.

Let me end this book with a fifth hymn, which I wrote myself as I was finishing this chapter. It can be sung to the tune of 'Just As I Am', and it sums up my experience in Iraq.

Oh, Reconcile Me Now to You!

Into the darkness I do go.
I long to see my Saviour's peace,
To see his light shining through.
Oh, reconcile me now to you!

I love you, Lord, I love you so,
Though I do see such conflict now.
I know your peace is deep within.
Oh, reconcile me now to you!

The bullets fly, the rockets thud.
I long, O Lord, to see you here,
To see your peace breaking through.
Oh, reconcile me now to you!

In every circumstance of life,
I know your peace does come with me
Despite the rampage all around.
Oh, reconcile me now to you!

I see your glory shining through.
The darkness fades at your command.
The glory heals the brokenness.
Oh, reconcile me now to you!

In this spirit I continue to fight for peace in the Middle East, and I will go on doing so until my Lord tells me to stop.

APPENDIX 1

WHO'S WHO

Abdel Latif Humayem, Sheikh Dr

In effect Saddam Hussein's personal imam, who wields great influence among the Sunna in Iraq. He visited America and Britain in 1999. After the war, he took refuge in Jordan, where he still lives. He returned briefly to Iraq in 2004 (and was greeted with great warmth by Ayatollah al-Sadr) but fled again when the National De-Ba'thification Committee seized all his wealth. In 2007, he introduced me to a member of al-Qa'ida in Amman. A delightful man, and one of the four authors of the Sunni/Shia fatwa against violence in 2008.

Abdel Qadir al-Ani, Sheikh Dr

The principal lieutenant in Iraq of Sheikh Dr al-Kubaisi, until he was obliged to flee to Jordan in 2004 after he was accused of being a traitor and his house was bombed. An important early ally.

Abu Ragif, Ayatollah Ammar

A senior lieutenant of Grand Ayatollah al-Sistani, who is also close to two of Iraq's four other grand ayatollahs. He has been a crucial ally – and a friend of Sheikh Dr Abdel Latif – since he joined us in Cairo in 2007. One of the four authors of the Sunni/Shia fatwa against violence in 2008.

al-Kubaisi, Sheikh Dr Ahmed

The most senior of Iraq's Sunna. He lives in Dubai, where he fled after falling out with Saddam many years ago, but exerts great influence in Iraq through his televized sermons. He joined us in Cairo in 2007, and was one of the four authors of the Sunni/Shia fatwa against violence in 2008.

al-Sadr, Ayatollah Hussein

The most senior Shia in Baghdad, an old friend of Dr Mowaffak and my closest spiritual ally in Iraq. He visited America and Britain in 1999, when I learned how his family had been decimated by the Ba'thists; but I found out only later how cruelly he himself had been tortured. A man of great holiness and wisdom, he was the 'father' of the Baghdad Religious Accord in 2004 and showed great warmth to Sheikh Dr Abdel Latif on his return to Iraq.

al-Sistani, Grand Ayatollah Ali

The most senior of Iraq's five grand ayatollahs, and the most powerful man in the country – his lieutenants told one of my colleagues, 'We are the government.' He lives in the holy city of Najaf and does not meet foreigners, but is said to approve strongly of our work. He endorsed the so-called Mecca Document in 2006, and his senior lieutenant Ayatollah Abu Ragif co-authored the Sunni/ Shia fatwa against violence in 2008.

al-Ubaidi, Sheikh Salah
The chief spokesman of Muqtada al-Sadr, he joined us in Cairo in 2008 and has since been a key ally, although he was not a signatory of the subsequent Sunni/Shia fatwa against violence.

al-Zuhairi, Sheikh Abdelhalim Jawad Kadhum
The chair of the gathering of Sunni and Shia scholars who signed the so-called Mecca Document in 2006 and chief religious adviser to Nuri al-Maliki since he became Prime Minister, who has worked with us since 2007. One of the four authors of the Sunni/Shia fatwa against violence in 2008.

Aziz, Tariq
Deputy Prime Minister of Iraq under Saddam, who first invited me to his country in 1999.

Bremer, Paul
The American administrator (or 'king') of Iraq from May 2003 to June 2004.

Carey, Dr George (later Lord)
The Archbishop of Canterbury from 1991 to 2002, when he was ennobled. He co-chaired the summit

that produced the Alexandria Declaration in 2002, having called all the delegates together, and sent me to Bethlehem later that year to try to help to resolve the siege of the Church of the Nativity. A kind and wise man, he became a very close friend and ally and was first chair and then patron of the Foundation for Relief and Reconciliation in the Middle East.

Coalition Provisional Authority (CPA)
The international (but overwhelmingly American) administration that ran Iraq from May 2003 until the handover of sovereignty in June 2004.

Fadel Alfatlawi
A member of my team in Baghdad immediately after the war, whom I first met as an exile in Coventry. In 2004 he succeeded Georges as secretary general of the Iraqi Institute of Peace, but he had to quit (and flee to Jordan) at the end of 2005 when the price on his head became too great.

Georges Sada
A former air vice-marshal in the Iraqi air force and a passionate Christian, whom I first met in Baghdad in 1999. He was my right-hand man in Iraq until he was headhunted to run its new Ministry of Defence in 2005. He was the first secretary general of the Iraqi Institute of Peace.

Hanna Ishaq
My man in Jerusalem, who has worked with me longer than anyone, first for the International Centre for

Reconciliation in Coventry and then for my Foundation for Relief and Reconciliation in the Middle East.

Hoyt, Colonel Mike

The most senior of the US Army chaplains in Iraq from 2006 to 2007 and a colleague in the Pentagon-funded work of the Iraqi Inter-Religious Congress.

Iraqi Institute of Peace (IIP)

The final name of the organization established by the Baghdad Religious Accord in 2004 to pursue peace and reconciliation in Iraq.

Maki, Peter

The young American who was the FRRME's director of operations from 2005 to 2007.

Mandeans

Adherents of a religion derived from the followers of John the Baptist.

Melchior, Rabbi Michael

The Deputy Foreign Minister of Israel from 2001 to 2002 and also (as it happens) the Chief Rabbi of Norway. One of my closest friends and co-workers for peace, whom I first met in 2001, when he suggested what was to become the Alexandria Process. An Orthodox Jew, he led the Jewish delegation in Alexandria and forged a crucial alliance – and friendship – with Sheikh Talal, with whom he shared the Coventry International Prize for Peace and Reconcilation with Patriarch Sabbah in 2002.

Mowaffak al-Rubaie, Dr
An old friend of Ayatollah al-Sadr whom I first met in 1999 in London, where he was living in exile and working as a neurologist. After the war, Paul Bremer appointed him to the Iraqi Governing Council and then gave him a five-year contract as Iraq's National Security Adviser. He is my principal adviser and one of my closest friends and allies in Iraq, and is the first chair of the Iraqi Institute of Peace. In 2008, he was awarded the FRRME's Prize for Peace in the Middle East.

Mukhabarat
The Arabic word for 'intelligence', and hence the name of Saddam's intelligence service.

Muqtada al-Sadr
The fiery young son of a grand ayatollah who was assassinated in 1999 by Saddam's agents, and the nephew of my dear friend Ayatollah al-Sadr. He commands Iraq's largest militia, the Shia Mehdi Army, which is a powerful opponent of both the multinational forces and al-Qa'ida in Iraq. His chief spokesman, Sheikh al-Ubaidi, joined us in Cairo in 2008 and has become a key ally.

Nuri al-Maliki
The leader of the (Shia) Da'wa Party, who became Prime Minister of Iraq in May 2007. He is a strong supporter of our work.

Petraeus, General David
The American commander of the multinational forces

in Iraq from January 2007 to September 2008, when he directed the so-called surge.

Ruth Heflin, Sister
The most forceful person I have ever met, who ran a charismatic church in Jerusalem and prophesied that my calling in life was to 'seek the peace of Jerusalem and the Middle East'.

Sabbah, Michel
The Latin Patriarch of Jerusalem, an Israeli Arab who led the Christian delegation in Alexandria. With Rabbi Melchior and Sheikh Talal, he was awarded the Coventry International Prize for Peace and Reconcilation in 2002.

Salah Tamari
The former PLO commander, then a member of the Palestinian Legislative Assembly, who led the first Palestinian negotiating team during the siege of the Church of the Nativity. He is now governor of Bethlehem.

Samia Aziz Mohamed, Mrs
The (Shia) Faili Kurd who chaired the IIP's working party on women, religion and democracy and herself became an MP.

Samir Raheem al-Sadooni
The former lawyer who was my driver in Baghdad immediately after the war and went on to become my

right-hand man in Iraq, first for the International
Centre for Reconciliation in Coventry and then as the
FRRME's director of Iraq. He also interprets for me.

Sawers, John
The British diplomat who as ambassador to Egypt in
2002 played a crucial part in the Alexandria Process. I
worked with him again in 2003 when he was Britain's
'special representative' in Iraq. He is now Britain's
ambassador to the United Nations.

Talal Sidr, Sheikh
A minister in the Palestinian Authority (though he
had been one of the founders of Hamas) who was
the inspirational leader of the Muslim delegation in
Alexandria. He forged a crucial alliance–and friendship
– with Rabbi Melchior, and shared the Coventry
International Prize for Peace and Reconcilation with
him and Patriarch Sabbah in 2002. He died in 2007.

Tantawi, Sheikh Muhammad Sayed
The Grand Imam of al-Azhar in Cairo, and as such
the highest authority in Sunni Islam. He was the co-
chair of the summit that produced the Alexandria
Declaration in 2002.

Wijdan Michael Salim, Mrs
An outstanding member of the Iraqi government who
is currently Minister for Human Rights. A Chaldean
Catholic who has become a very good friend of mine.

Yazidi

Members of an ancient community concentrated in northern Iraq who revere an angel sometimes called Shaytan and hence are often (wrongly) regarded by Muslims as Devil worshippers. In 2007, almost 800 were killed by suicide bombers in two co-ordinated attacks.